Twin Passions

Photographs & Poems

Coleen Marks

Publisher: PrintPOD Publishing
Hillsborough, New Jersey

Editor: Jacqueline Flamm
Production Coordinator: Michael Aslett
Production Editor: Kymberly Rosenthal

Contact: printpodpub@gmail.com
Phone: 908-917-3400

Printed in the United States of America

First Edition 2020

ISBN: 978-0-578-66580-1

Dedication

For Marvin
whose infinite patience and poses
made all this possible

Contents

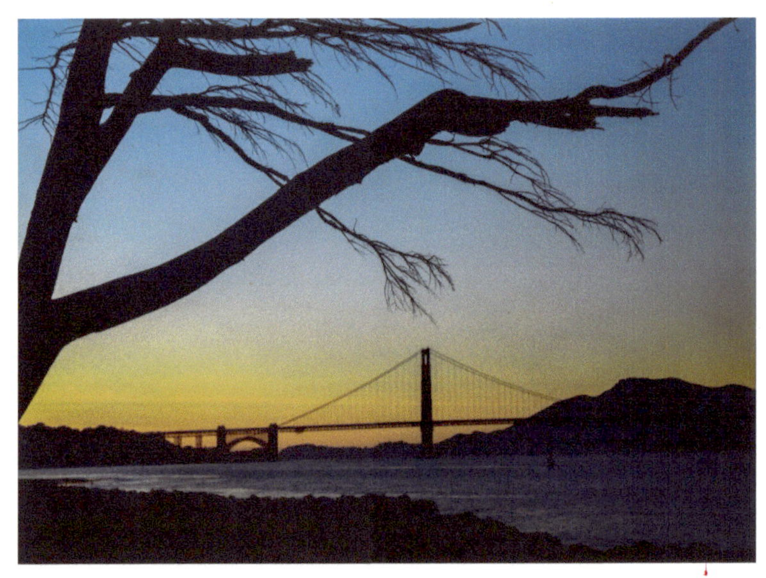

Last Light

Running down the beach
camera chasing last light
full of silhouettes

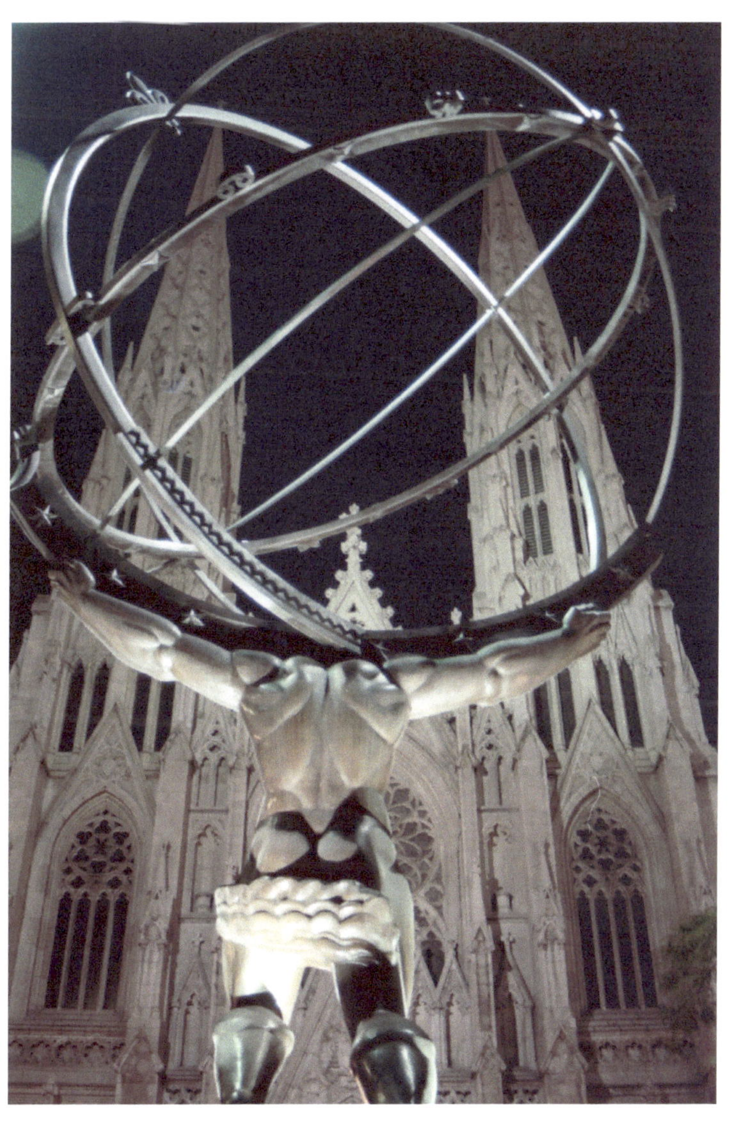

Atlas

Lifted to heaven
gothic spires look down upon
the weight of the world

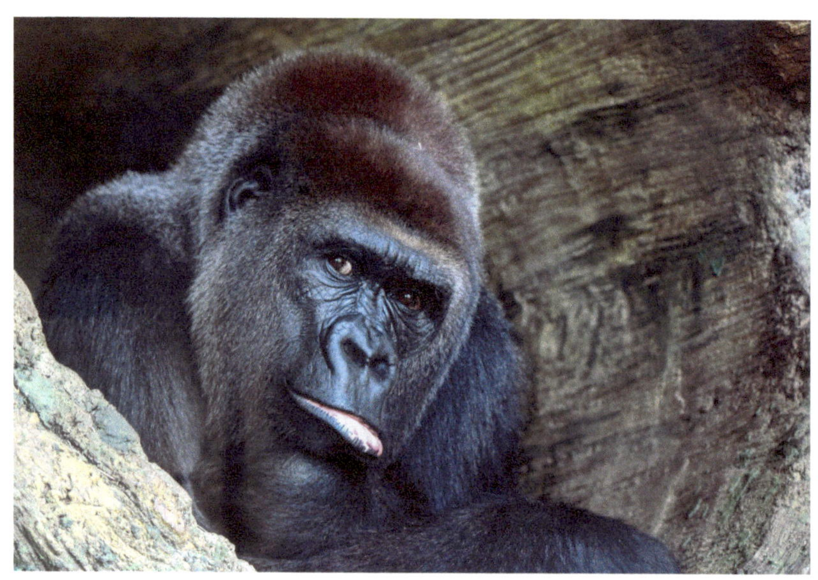

Chicago Gorilla

Photographers carry
their camera everywhere.
Look through the lens to
catch brief capsules of time.
To freeze events before they can go
down the rabbit hole of memory.
But most of all, for the adventure,
the possibility that one image
might haunt, might rise to art.

On this day we went to the zoo.
That region of faraway animals.
It's what you do on vacation
with a grandchild. And we
wander into the land of the gorilla,
his hairy hulk slumps
against the glass of his
modern windowed "habitat"
designed by caring zookeepers.

But what does a wild creature
from the warm rain-soaked danger of jungles
know of Chicago winters, extinction.
His elbow resting on a rock
we are face to face and
he looks me straight in the eye
with a deep wordless stare, *I see you,*
then turns his head.

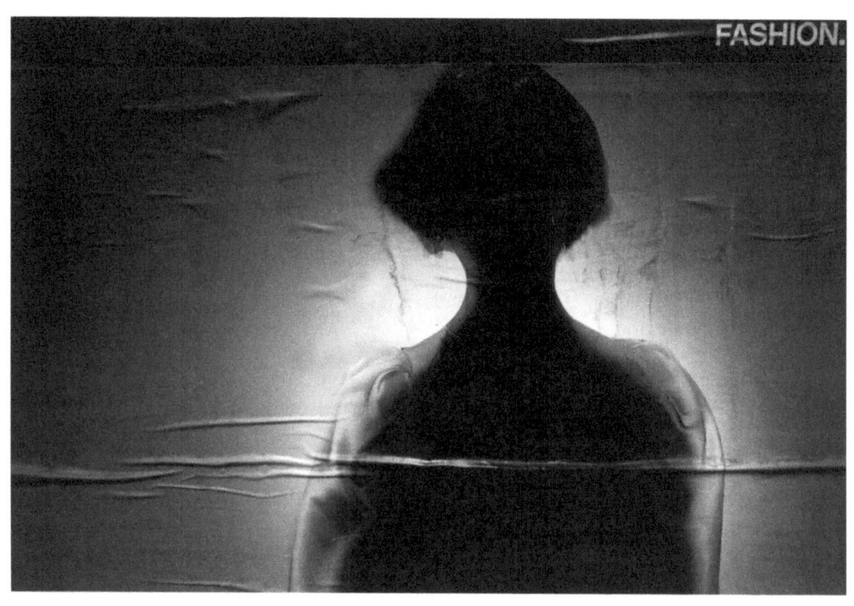

FASHION.

Fashion

Just a wrinkled poster
plastered on a construction wall
under an eerie walkway.
Captured while I wandered
on a theatre district night.

Just a grab shot. My life always
a circus in search of a tent,
all my photos on the move,
caught from the corner of the eye.

A woman's backlit faceless head
glowing yellowish gray and black
so tightly cropped only one word
is left of the message FASHION.

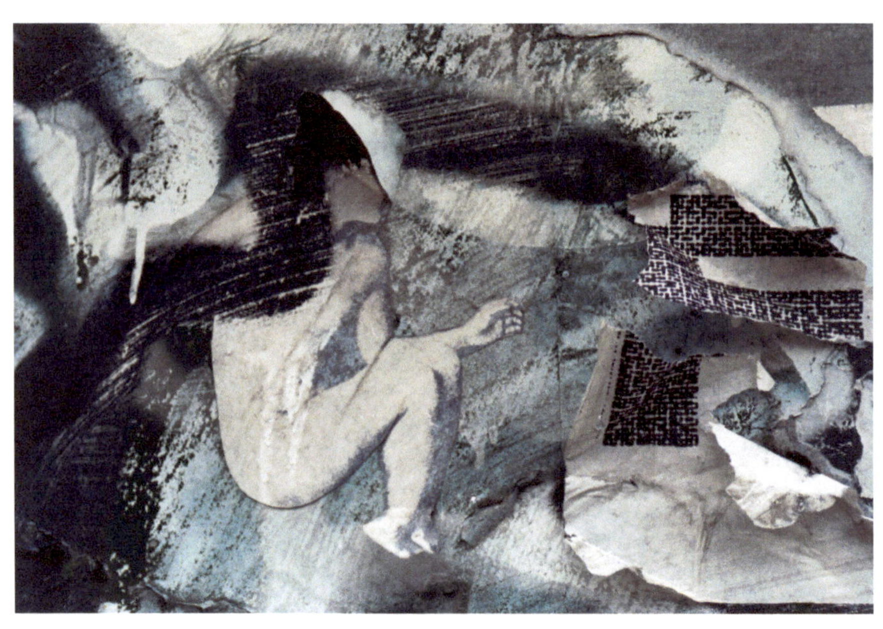

Found Art

You see it only
if you want to
are looking for
torn edges.

The black swish
of a paint can
that paper lifting
on the right.

A curled blue-edged man
his hand reaching out
face turned away
like Adam.

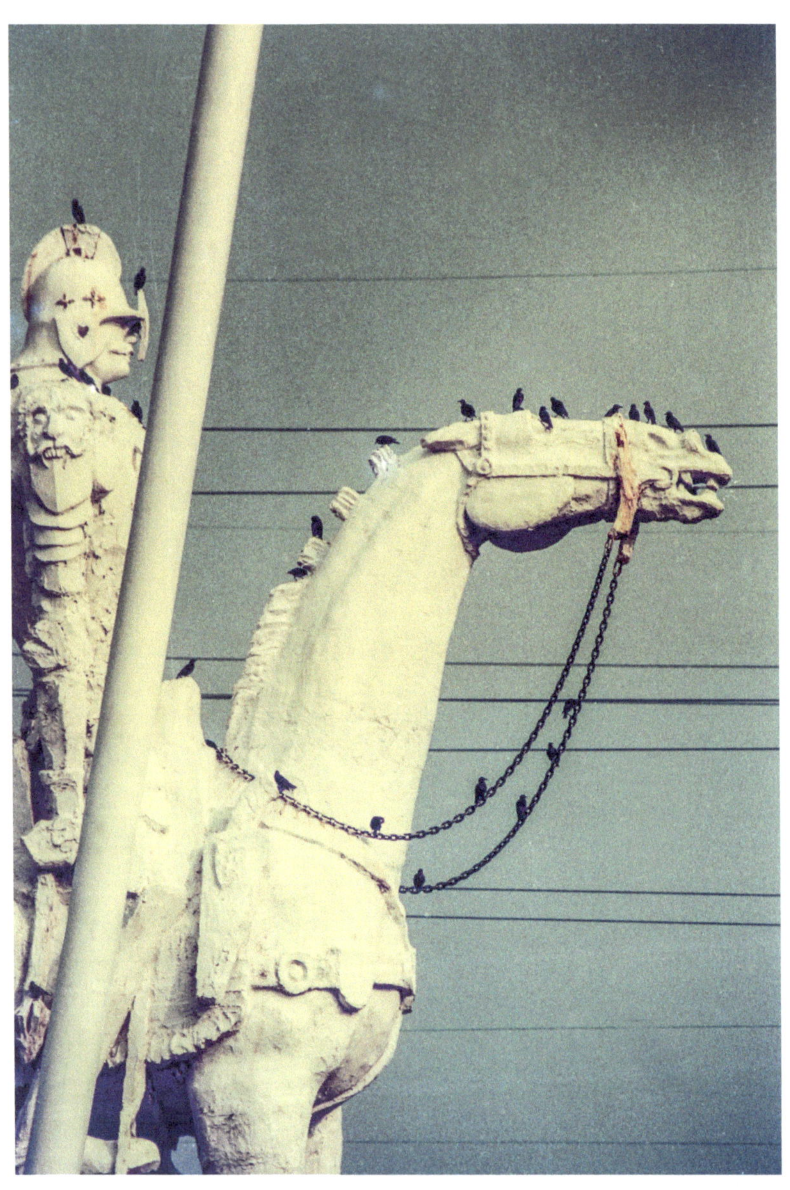

For the Birds

The statue crumbled, now
totally gone, a true white knight,
over thirty feet high
standing out in the field
like a specter. Created
to honor a Polish patriot's
valiant medieval ancestry.

Early one morning, my camera
caught a flock of tiny birds
sitting on the horse's head,
the knight's helmet, and
arrayed upon the reins
like notes of music.

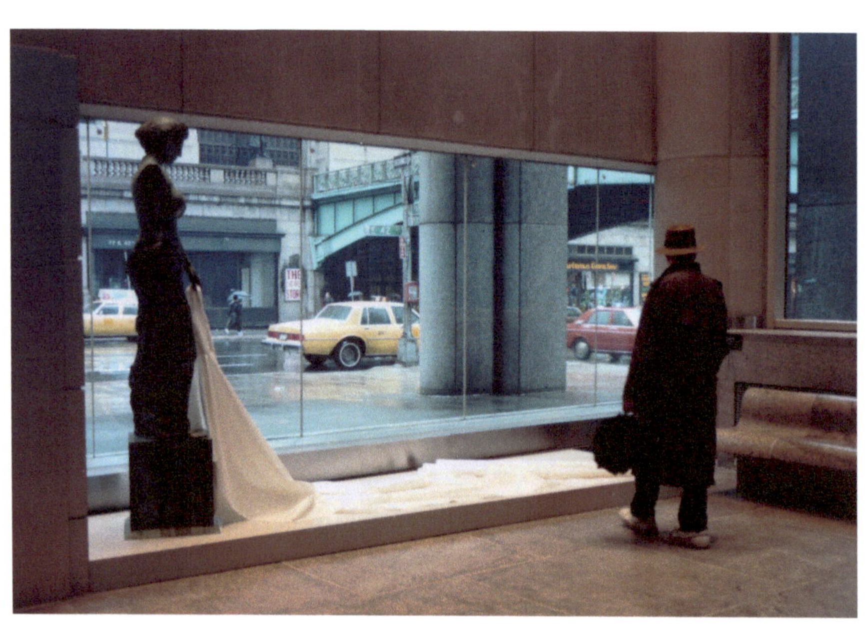

Window Dressing

Remembering, verbatim, an unpublished poem
is the most dreaded of the ten disciplines
in the World Memory Championships.

Our human brain knows
its recall faculties finite,
neural nets hard-wired
to never dwell upon the words
just, what does it all mean.

And while our metaphors are
hanging clever curtains, our brains
are staring out the window
searching for the story.

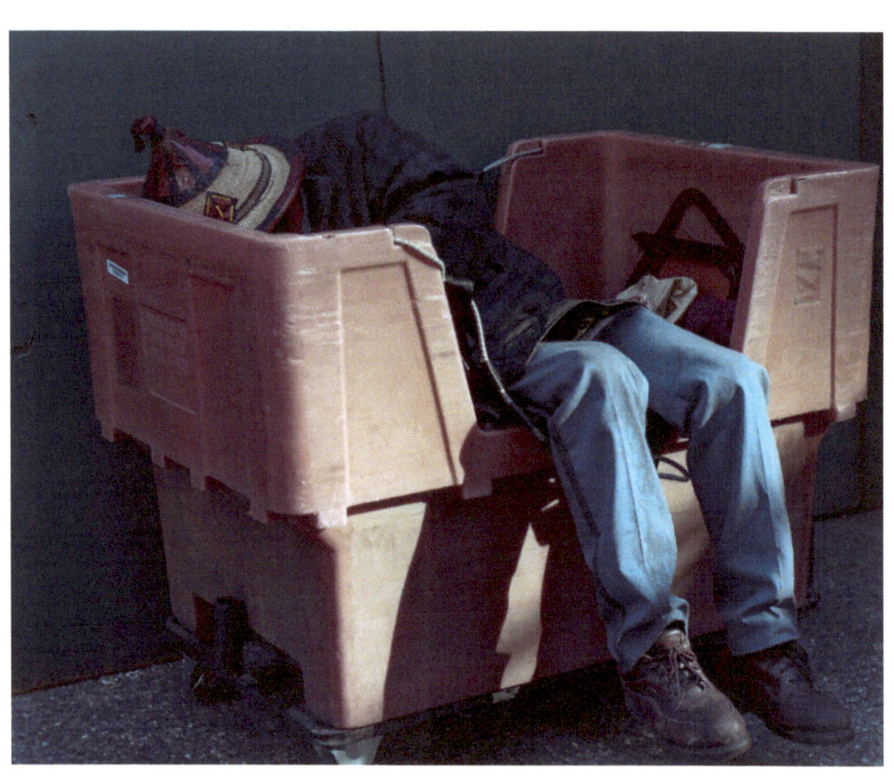

Rubbish

In this late afternoon light
full of slanted shadows
you tucked asleep
cramped like that
in a rolling rubbish bin.
Your small legs dangling
like blue-jean vines
against its earthy orange.

How does it come to this?
Did your decisions slip
the net of home
tough-loved out of reach?
Or have you escaped a house
so strewn with abuse and neglect
your tears finally left for the street?

Cradled on this garbage
do you sleep peacefully
away from the dilemmas
of a pocket-change life?
Dream of a love that
cannot bear your absence?
Or, are you listening to our
footsteps as we pass by, leave you
on the great bottom of this city.

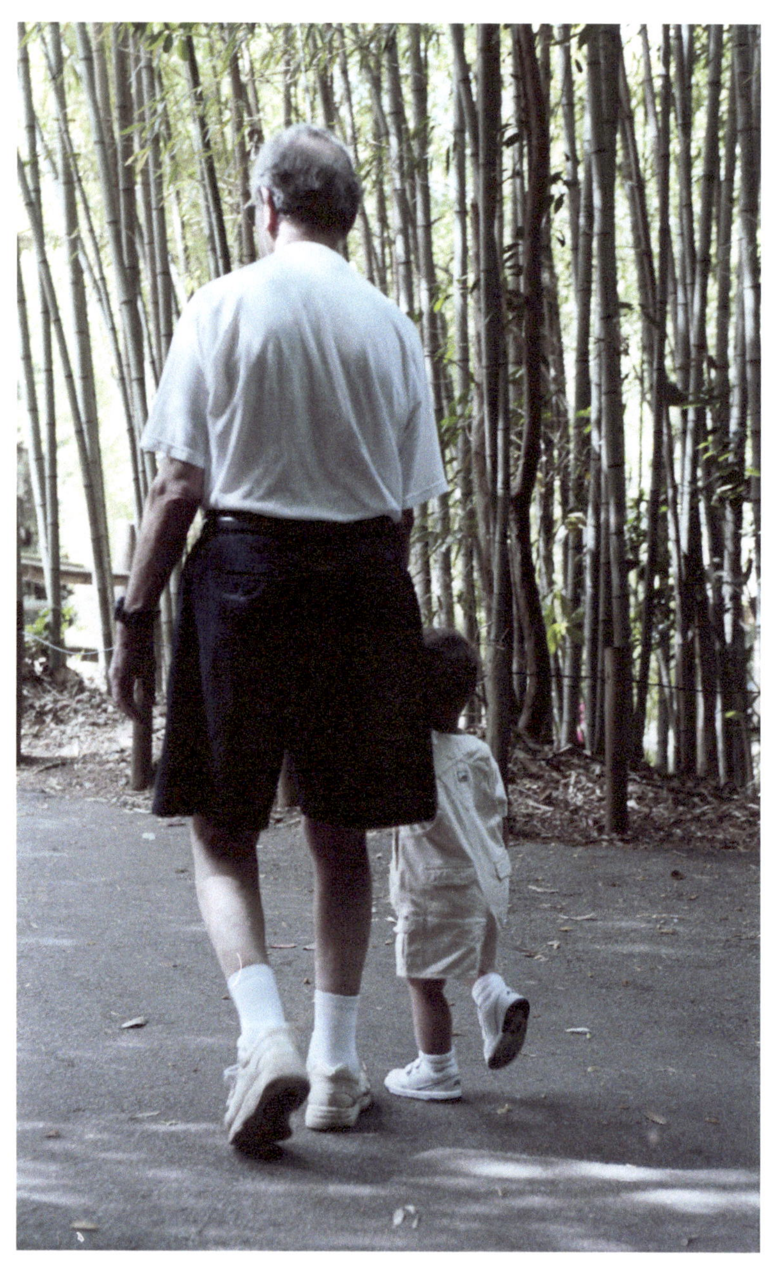

Note to Grandson

You become a teen on this birthday
and we wish for you resilience
as you feel your hormones rising,
the ever pressures of making high grades,
learn the awkward truths of superficial friends,
and enter the unavoidable darkness
of rebellions ahead.
We unleveled the playing field
as we watched you try on your life
providing euphonium lessons,
a brown belt in Karate,
summer camp cartooning.
Helped with memberships at the
Met, MoMA and the Philadelphia Museum,
trips to seven National Parks,
five historic battlefields, two President's homes,
and all of Washington, DC.
Took you to visit sea life at the Georgia Aquarium,
Sue the dinosaur at the Field Museum,
and all those strange animals at many zoos.
To see *Matilda* and *Hamilton* on Broadway.
Yet, more important,
we ask tough questions like,
Is this behavior going to
get you what you want?
Make time to really listen
as we try to keep your baggage light.
Often point to our sign on the wall
that says, *Someone else is happy*
with less than what you have.

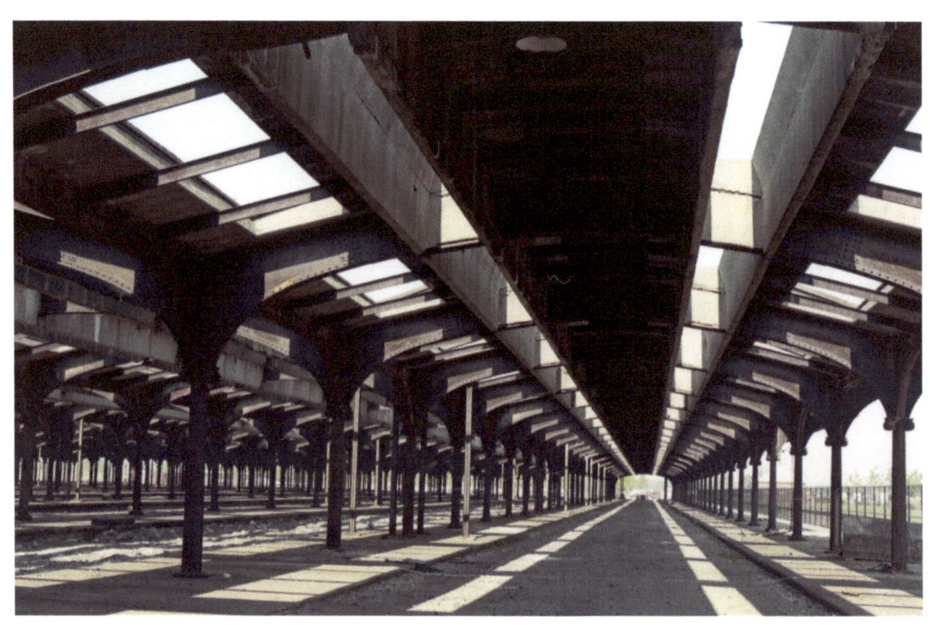

Station

Long gone are the trains
teeming with our relatives
from Ellis Island

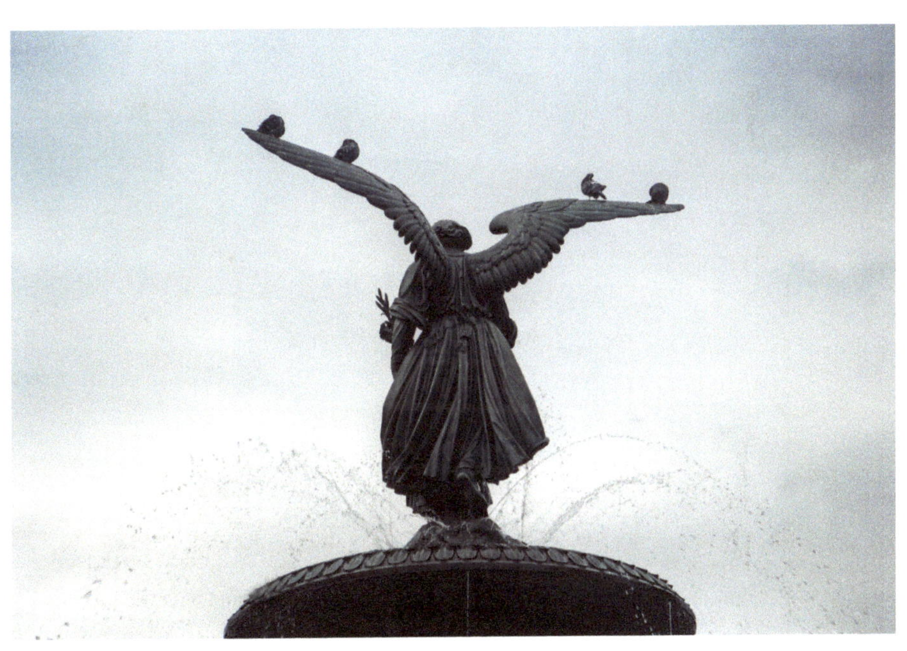

Bethesda

Angel wings spread wide
a famous fountain for a
city pigeon roost

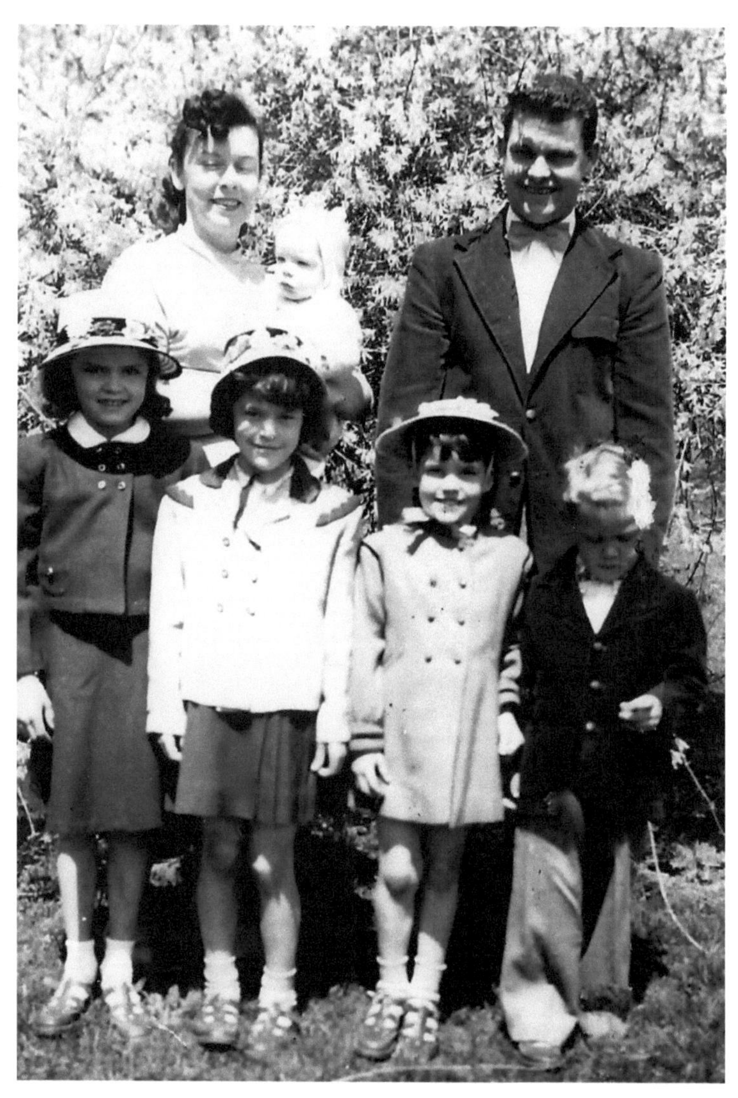

Our Tenor
for Danny

Child number five.
I changed your diapers,
threw water on the fire
you started in the kitchen garbage,
felt my mouth agape when
your Irish tenor *Danny Boy*
sang out across the huge
auditorium at All-State.
But then, those alcoholic years,
the tears until you surfaced,
told us you had been singing in
a famous Atlanta Baptist church
after we thought you lost.
I remember veiled answers
always shrouded our talks.
Your headstrong heart always
deep into the latest self-help cure.
But you were beyond
paperback remedies
always searching for that
carefree river summer
of beer and lobsters.
I sat beside your hospital bed
as you told me it was time
to turn the page
put your own name on it.
Let go the tether of dialysis,
the pain, and leave before
you could forget where you
left the keys, must lose your legs

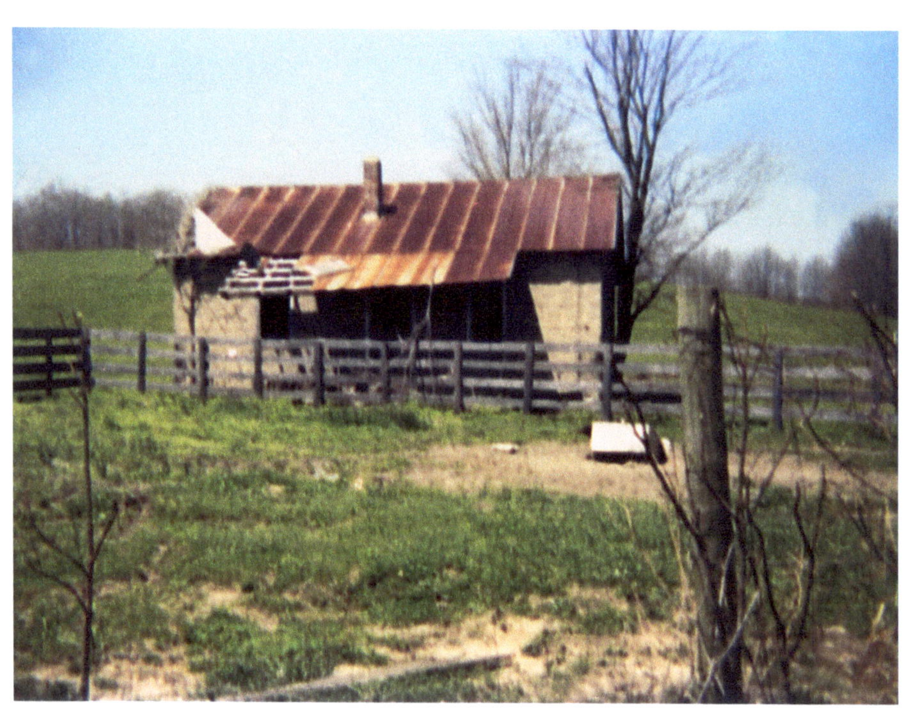

This is Ben's Eldest

for Benjamin Franklin Marks

Waiting outside the change house
to carry your lunch pail home
I remember all those miners' black faces
pouring out of the lift.
Your tales of childhood in the hardscrabble
sharecropping South.
First and always a carpenter, how you taught me the many
different kinds of wood as we rubbed the beauty in.
But most of all your humor right to the end,
when you told my sister, *Don't buy the shovel yet!*

The silence came so quickly, for one just sixty-six.
Cancer on Valentine's Day, gone by Memorial Day.
This dying a most singular thing, and one
more day too much when the pain comes.
Knowing the crop was lost, you said it was enough
and went down under that rich dark soil
you were always looking for, leaving behind
just the usual things: jackets on hooks, shoes in a closet,
pocket knife, photographs in a wallet, seven children
and your smile on my face.

And I finally visit your stories down in this
Tennessee River valley, where time and dust
float slowly in the southern heat.
Our family gathers bringing dishes they are known by.
And cousins say, *You're okay for a Yankee, cause your kin.*
They all hear slower than I speak so
I repeat myself to these familiar unknown faces.

Next day, Uncle Doug's Chevy pick-up
carries us down narrow dirt roads as he
explains how he got the *calling* to preach at revivals
and I smile my Northeastern smile.
We pull up to the beginning
a tin roofed sharecropper's shack
leaning like age near Bluewater Creek
and Uncle Doug says, *Over yonder there's*
Brown Wilson's fields where your daddy worked
his last crop before going North,
and I feel that rich dark soil of dreams,
that lowdown cool of creeks.

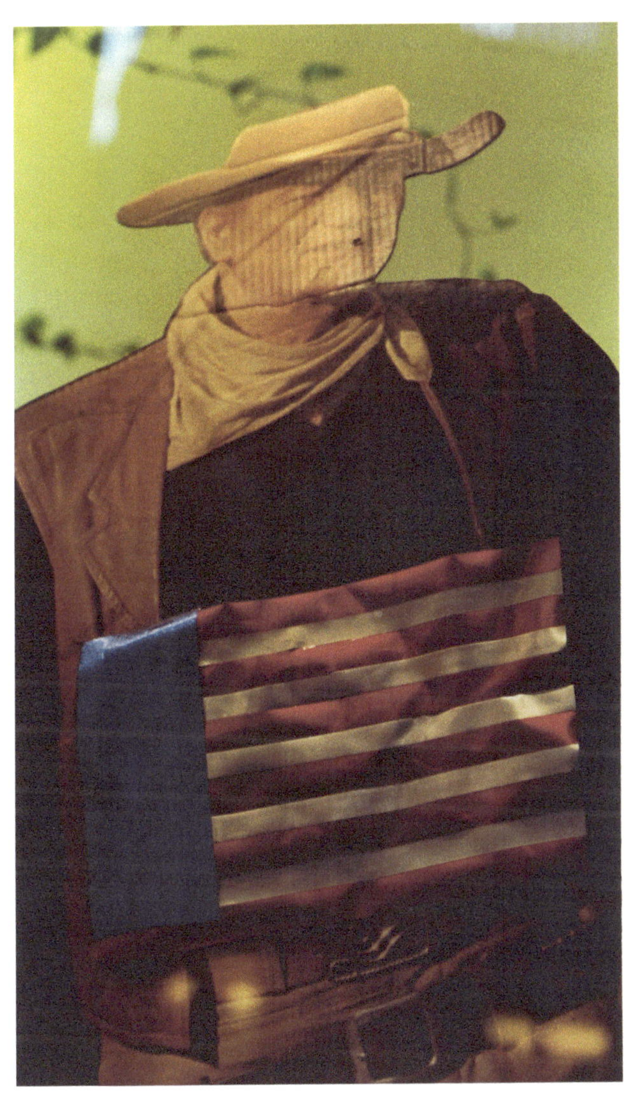

John Wayne

Always riding tall
a courageous straight shooter
real lives much harder

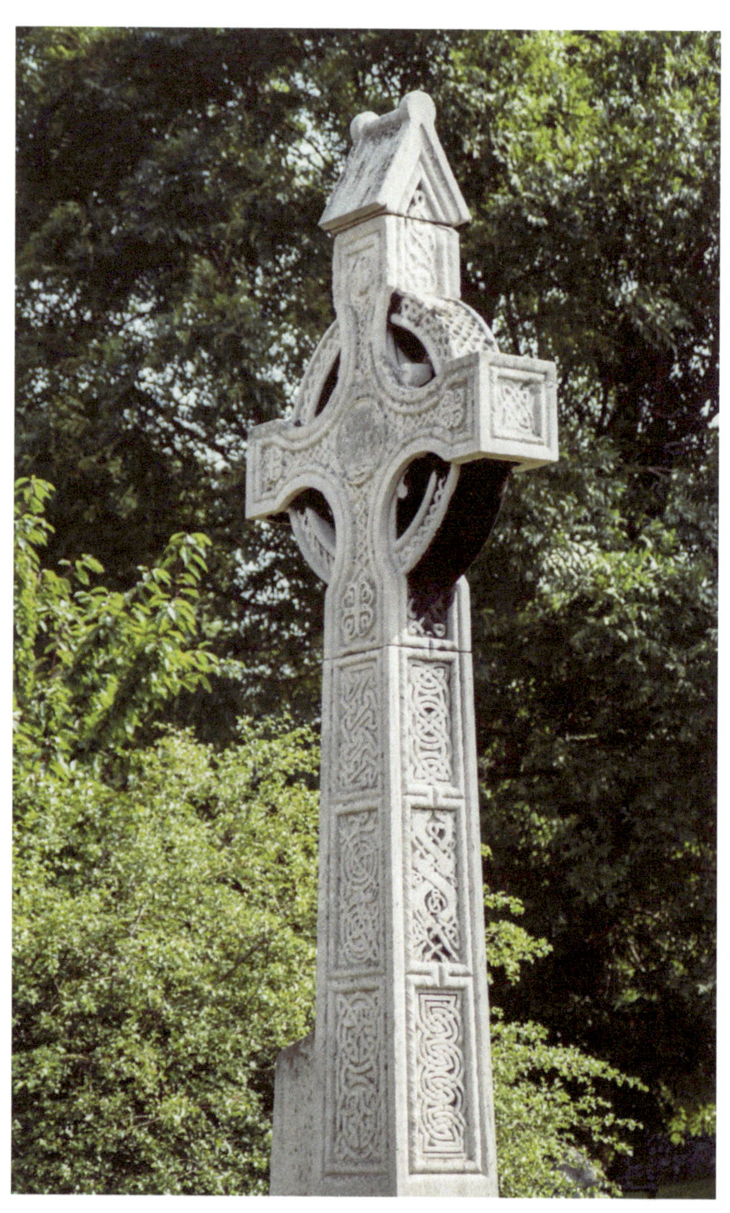

Heritage

All our lines start long, then uniquely rearranged.
I am 86.4% Irish from the Potato Famine
5.3% French/German from Medieval scholars
1% Spanish from the Armada and .4% Scandinavian
from the marauders. All of us they say
from a seminal mother in Africa.

I am strong from the Mullen Clan
of fierce warrior women. Know Brooklyn
brownstones, outhouses and open mineshafts
with rich magnetic iron ore deep below.

I am from foot-tapping banjos
and skillet cornbread, gathering
eggs and slopping hogs. Summers on
fire escapes, Italian ices and pink
Spaulding's off stoops. I am from
Macy's and Coney Island,
shotguns and venison. Daddy's
pungent pickle recipe.

I know the Beatitudes, can sing
Kyrie Eleison, McNamara's Band,
Take an Old Cold Tater and Wait.

I am from, *your time will come*
and *patience is a virtue,*
all the pieces that need me to exist
for the past to recognize itself.

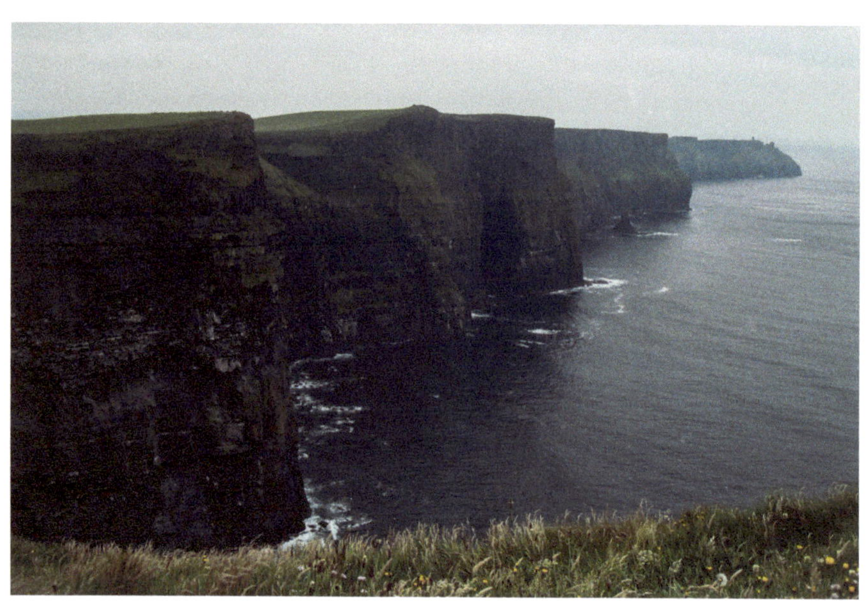

Tales of Irish Luck

With two toddlers in the backseat, crawling
in twin lanes of construction traffic, the old
Plymouth's water pump steams and expires
and we are hood-up-stranded, when inching
in the other lane appears a food truck, its shirt-torn
driver discerning our plight resolves our need
for water, then apologizes for his shabby attire
and I say, *You look like an angel to me.*

Then there's the incident along early morning
Route 1, when my Honda's tire rumbles flat.
Forever running late, and not my first rodeo, I pull out
the tools, but the lug nuts have been tightened
by Hercules, when calmly strolling out of the woods
comes a man in a business suit, briefcase in hand.
We dispense with the tire and he explains his home
is back in those woods and he likes to walk
to work at his bank just down the road.

We once had an *unsafe-at-any-speed* VW Beetle
which on our neat suburban street nearing home
began to sputter and behind the rear window,
where the engine famously is, I see flames shooting up.
I urgently pull over and jump out, when
a cable guy runs toward me with
a fire extinguisher, he explains later
they all carry in their trucks.

Still, I have not given up my membership in AAA.

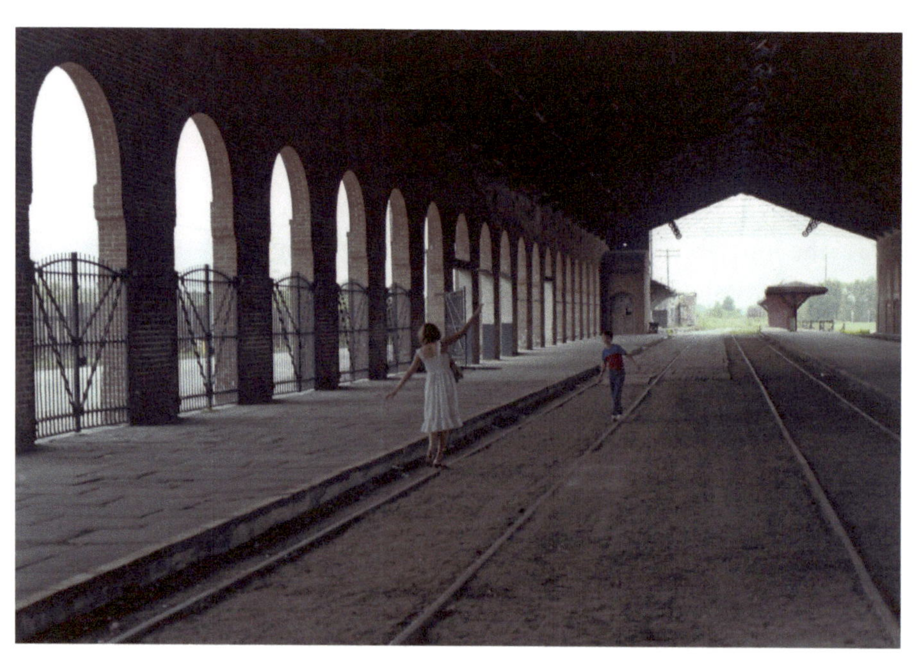

Oh, Grow Up

I know I must break
my promise to Peter Pan
relinquish x-ray vision
flying the Millennium Falcon
leave Never-Never-Land
where only the crocodile
has a clock.

But there is a plan
hanging on a hook
inside my vacant stares
for a few more heroic
races, catches, songs,
where once again
I am carelessly alive.

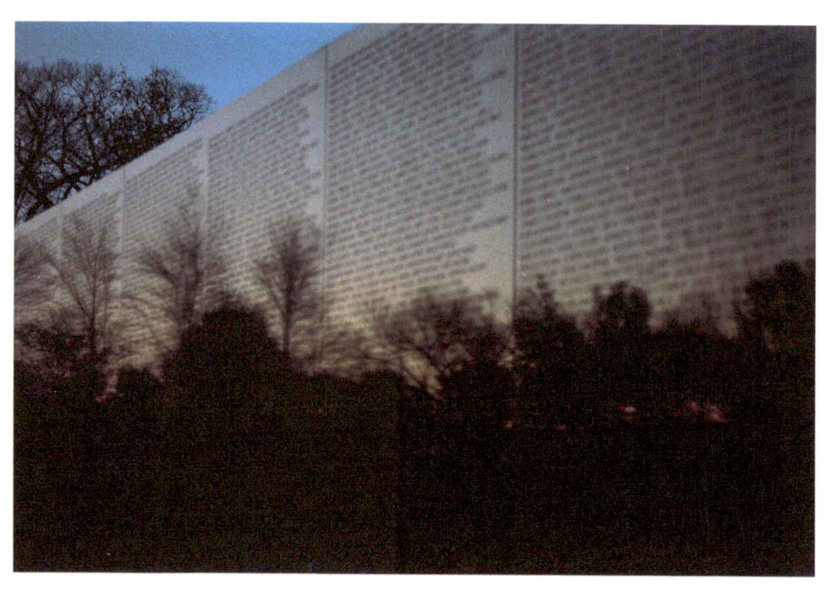

Sgt. Gomez

We all called him *Spanky*
for he was short like his father
lost forever down a mineshaft
when he was just a twig
that grew a little wild
and his single mother thought
the Army just the thing for pruning.
He left early when seventeen
whip smart and muscular
I just fourteen with girlhood
wafting on a flirting breeze.
And the Army was just the thing
for it became his father
gave him brothers and a war.
His breeze came briefly by again.
Now I was seventeen
of more shapely interest
to a seasoned ranger
on assignment to West Point
teaching fresh lieutenants
how to wage a jungle war.
Too soon he followed duty back
was lost on some
nameless numbered hill
they had taken once before.

Now a breeze is blowing down
this long black granite wall
I find I never knew
your first name was Gelasio.

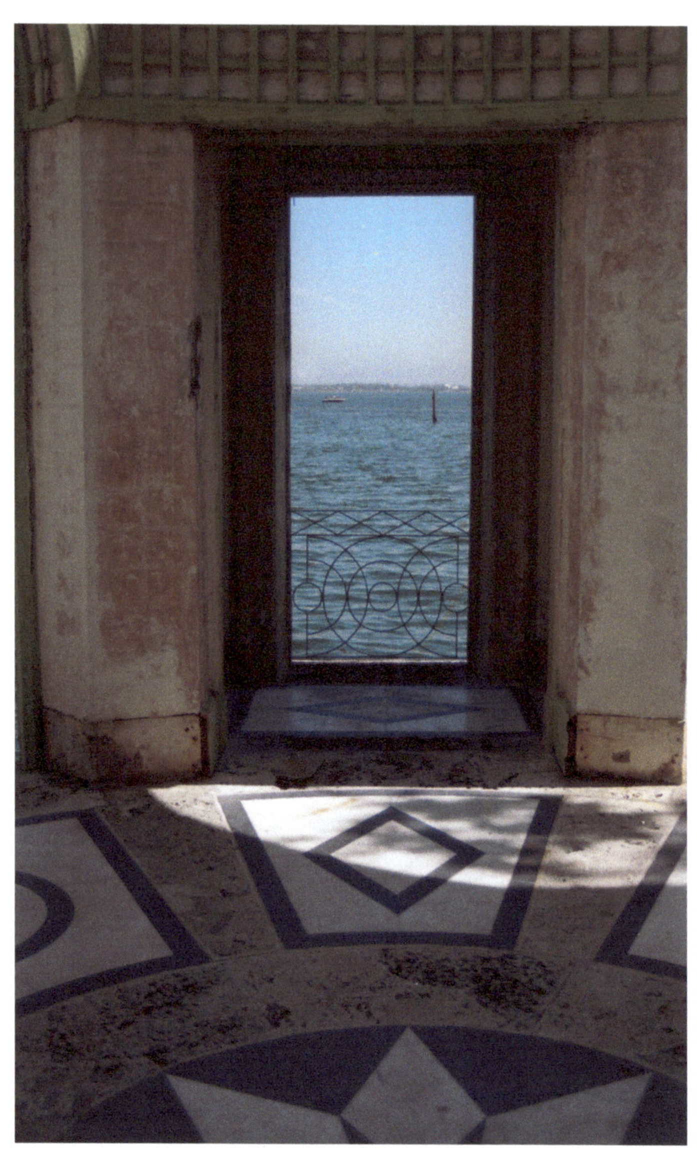

Patterns

Shadows and sunlight
a gazebo holds open
the door to the sea

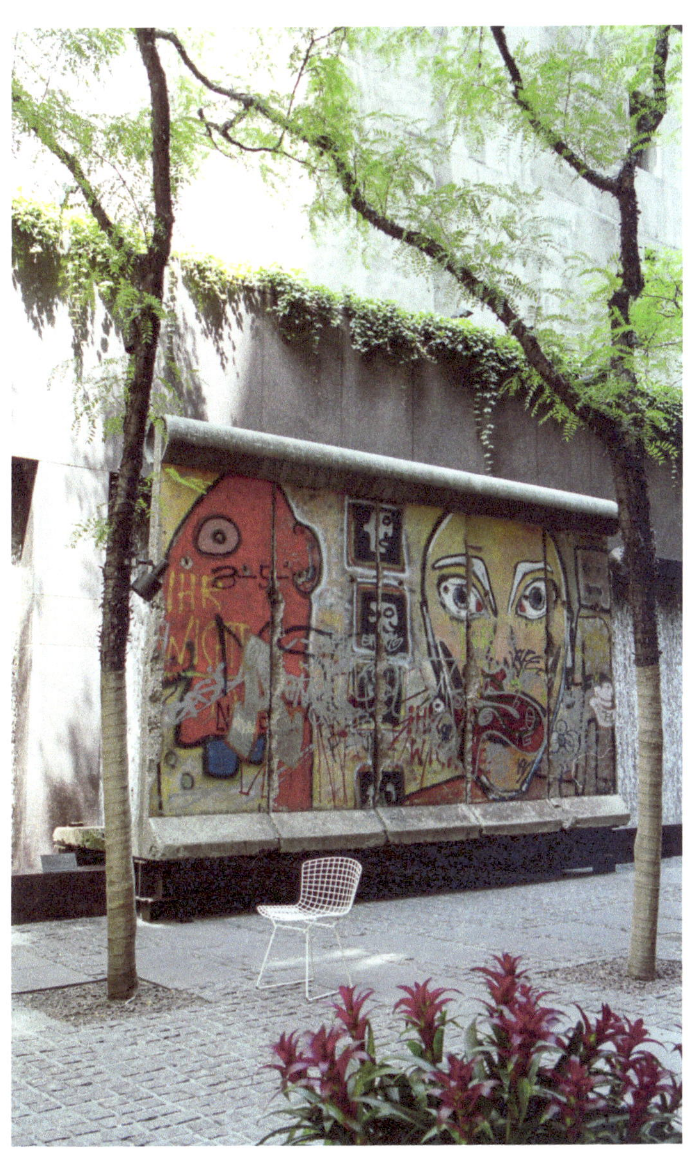

The Wall

New York pocket park
section of painted concrete
message from Berlin

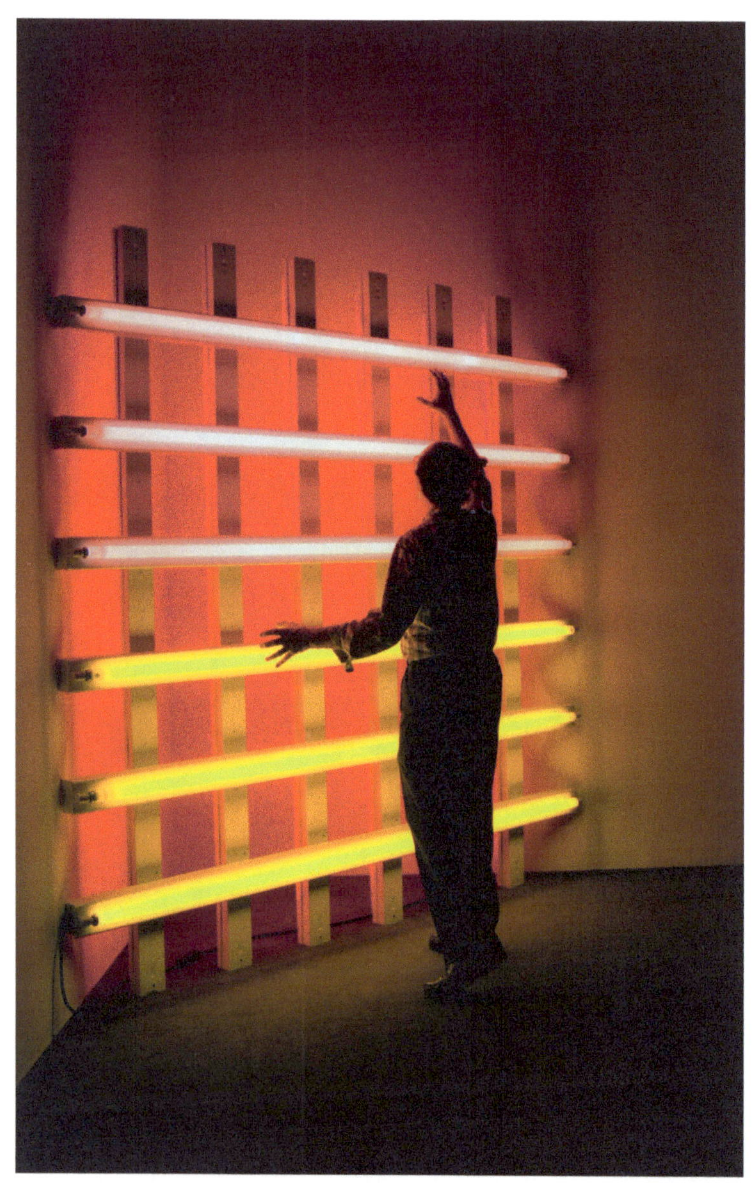

A Poet Goes to Business

The credenza is curious.
It suspects you're in disguise
here on an inside job
hidden behind this desk.

Even your silk flowers know
that personnel folders are
too small to hold a human spirit.
That org charts can't make leaders.

Daily brainstorms cross the sea
of information, computers flood
with emails, while cool fluorescence
watches us walk the talk, climb the ladder.

For this poet, it's all just musical
chairs, the corner office an illusion,
as we paperwork through year
after year of small print.

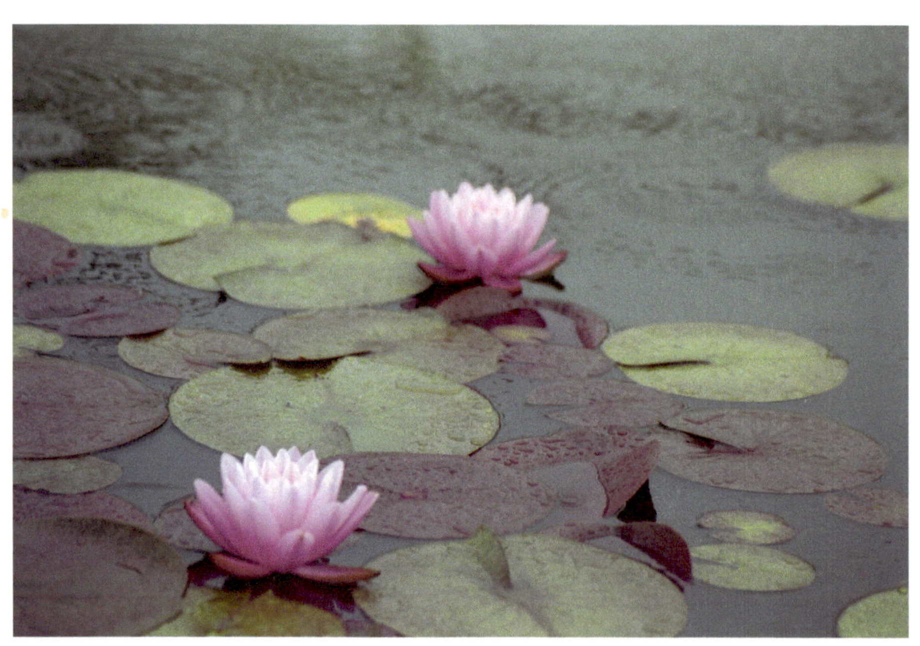

Civilities

for Misty

First - do no harm.

I am without incantations
for your terminal disarray.
Time, quiet as a wristwatch
is suddenly Big Ben
in this now short story,
the one where you die.

And how do you speak to
the end of a story?
Conversation is a sea,
you must keep moving, stay afloat
but our words grow heavy
sink into silences.

Today, with no forward,
I reach back into the corners
of our music, our poetry
as the day becomes a split screen
of grief and work and I demand
some gesture from the sky,
some gray, some rain.

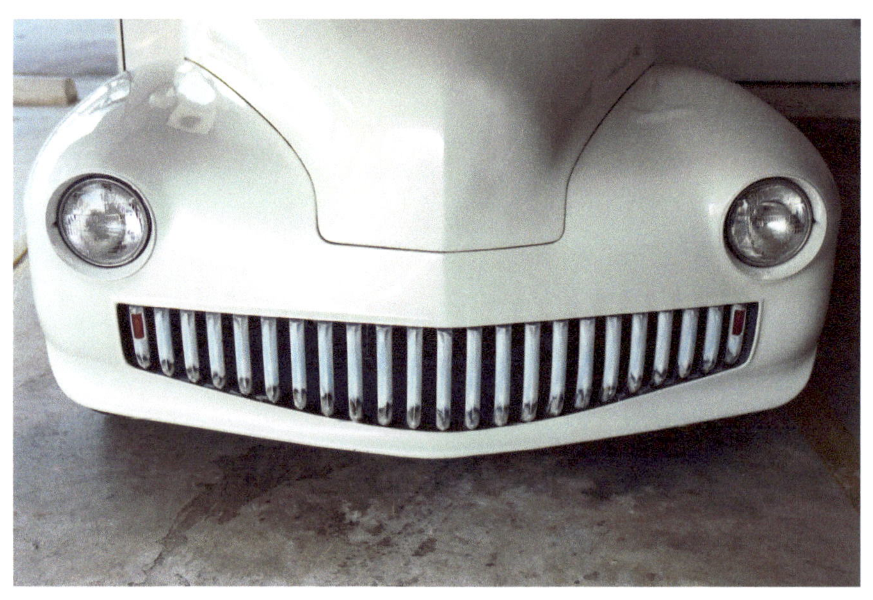

The Visits, 1969

For Alice Mullen

I went often to visit
my witty Grandmother
who ended up
down a long hall
in one shared room
with a number,
seldom encountering
other visitors.

A stroke back in the day
when doctors were in the dark
and she was robbed
of the whole side of herself,
most terribly, of speech.

She loved to fly away
from that room.
I would place my two
noisy toddlers on her lap
and we'd all go for a ride
up and down the hallways
through the gauntlet
of parked patients
tied with sheets
to their wheelchairs
who would lift their
heads and smile.

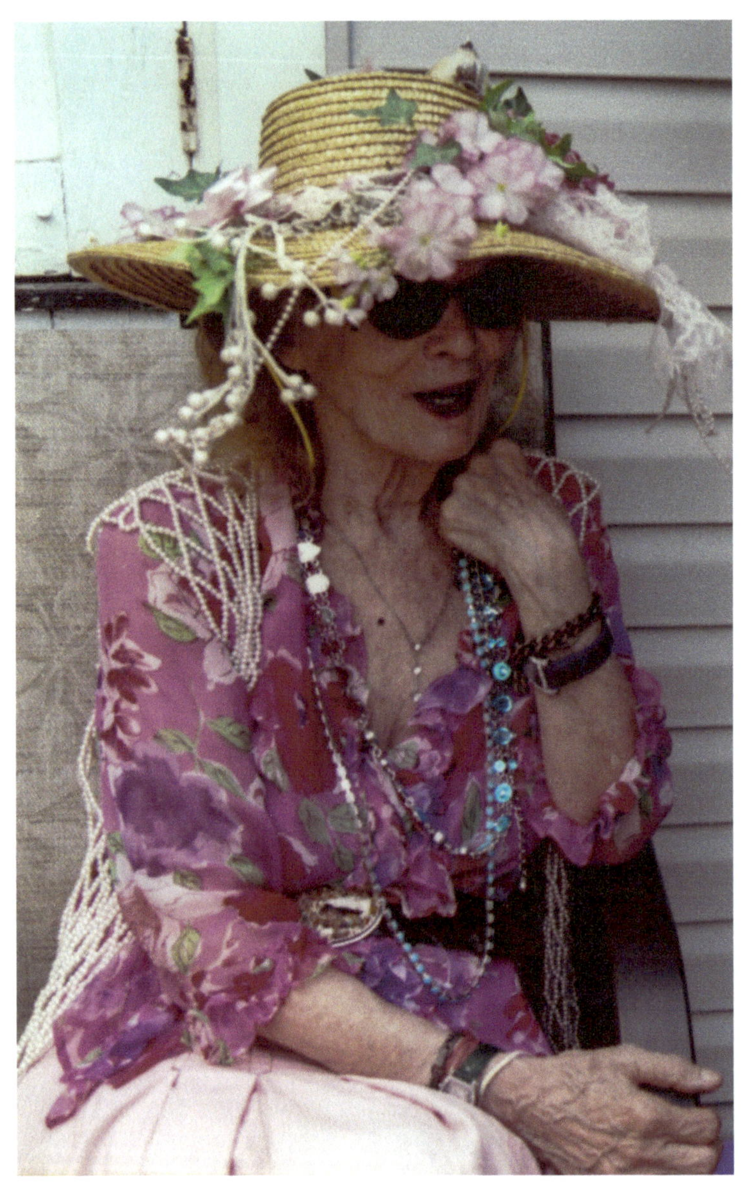

Today is Bloom's Day

for Evelyn

It is sunrise on our street
of postwar ranch houses
young City marrieds first purchased
with a VA mortgage and two dollars down.
My time for a walk.
When I see her Barbie-painted face
sitting on the neighbor's lawn
reading their newspaper.

In her driveway next to mine
sits a VW bus the Collyer brothers
could have left there and
her scrawny cat sits posed in
an Egyptian prayer for food.
She approaches wearing an
unknown Picasso wrapping her
heart of gold. This morning
she recites Tennyson,

Break, break, break
On thy cold grey stones, O Sea!
And would that my soul could utter
The thoughts that arise in me.

Then speaks to me with eyes
that peer through a gypsy's glass
I'm nervous, she says,
Today is Bloom's Day and
I'm to read from Ulysses at the college.
I say, *Yes, again yes, I understand, yes.*

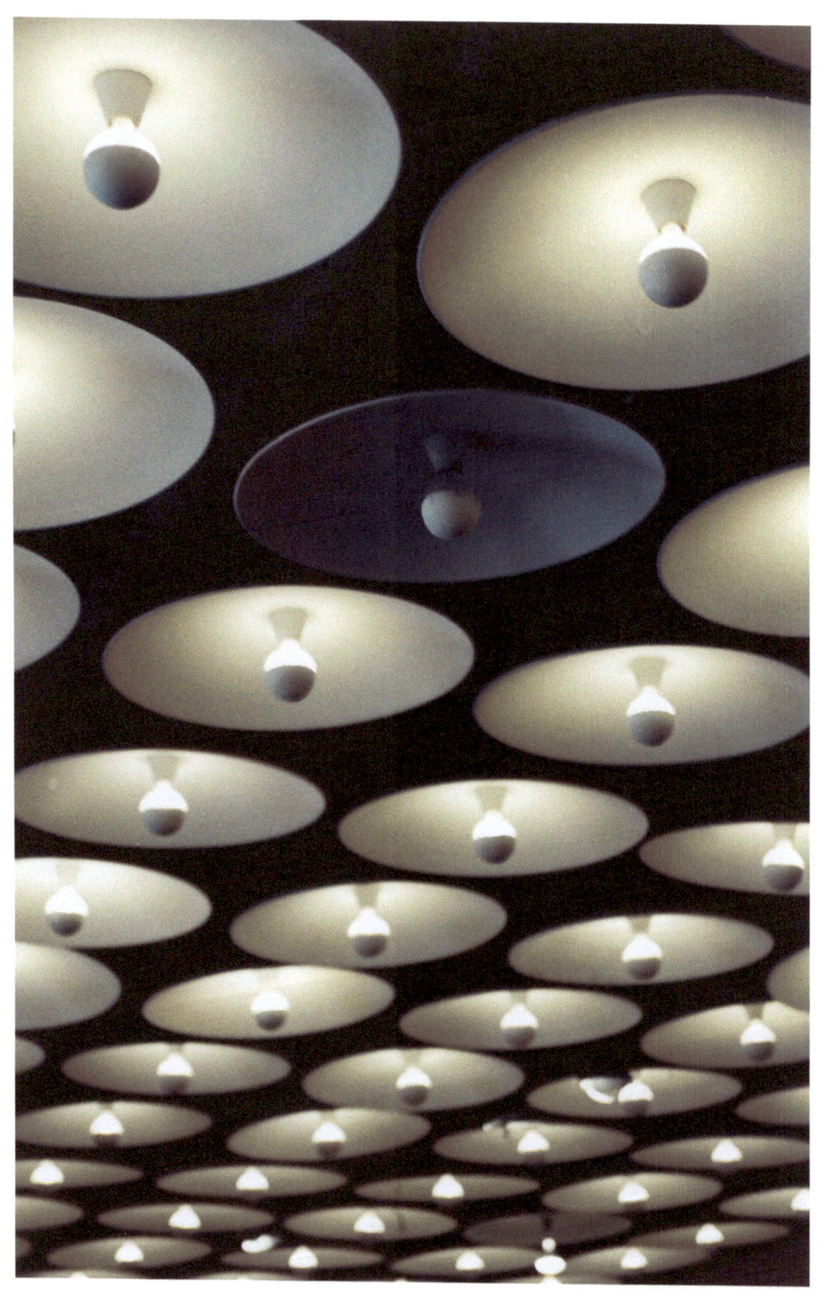

The Black Sheep

And now, how far you have come
from your clan cannot be undone.

Maybe it was because you had
left the cult of the Virgin
to undress for paintings,
the breath of hot kisses
in the bruised smell of mint.
Married a Jew.

Or, being the oldest gave you a
distance put you in charge,
your father's right hand.
Plus you had always hated their gossip,
had made a pact with Peter Pan,
your face always lost in a book.

Or, found you could never really network
with those who bought the ladder,
kept their lives in resumes,
could not see past the bottom line,
believed bank books were
the true measure of worth.

Or then, because you became Joe Friday,
trying to sort out Rashomon,
searching for words with answers
somewhere out on the edge.

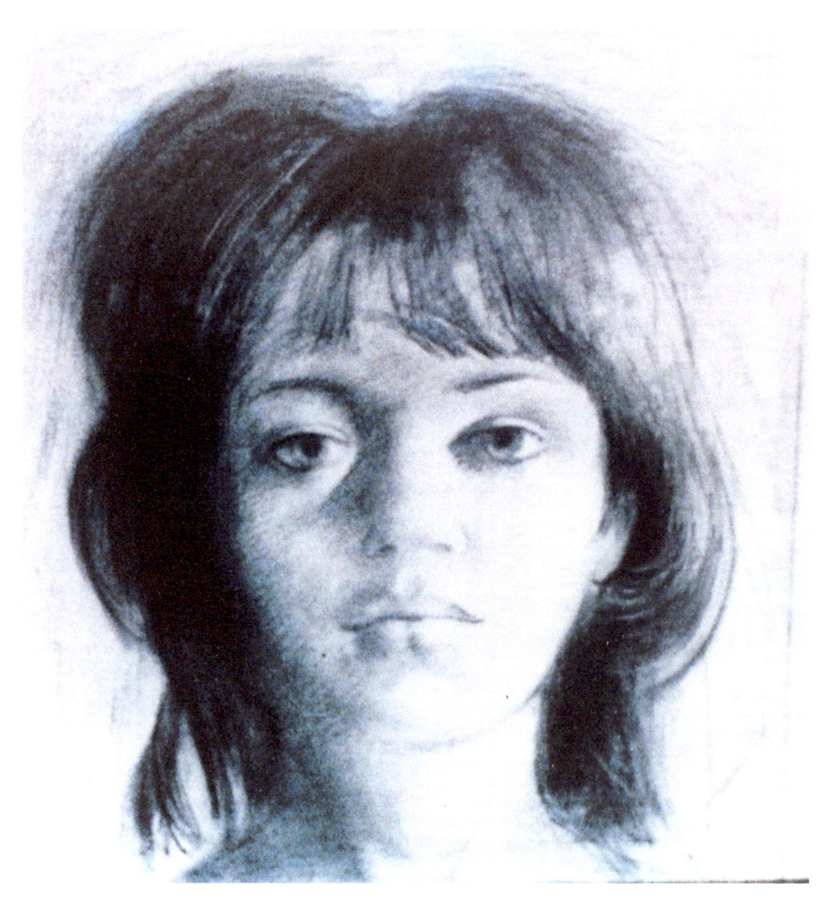

The Studio

I still smell how strong they were,
the paints, gum turpentine.
Light entered from the north
so charcoal shadows would
not change upon my face
as he caught it, pensive, true
with his Rembrandt eyes.

Light faded, blurred to evening
then slid from the canvas as
alizarin crimson squeezed up
hard against the cap
to fly off at his touch.

The picture hung now on my wall
warms faintly still with ardor.
And sipping wine out of Waterford
I try to recall what else it was
I thought I needed.

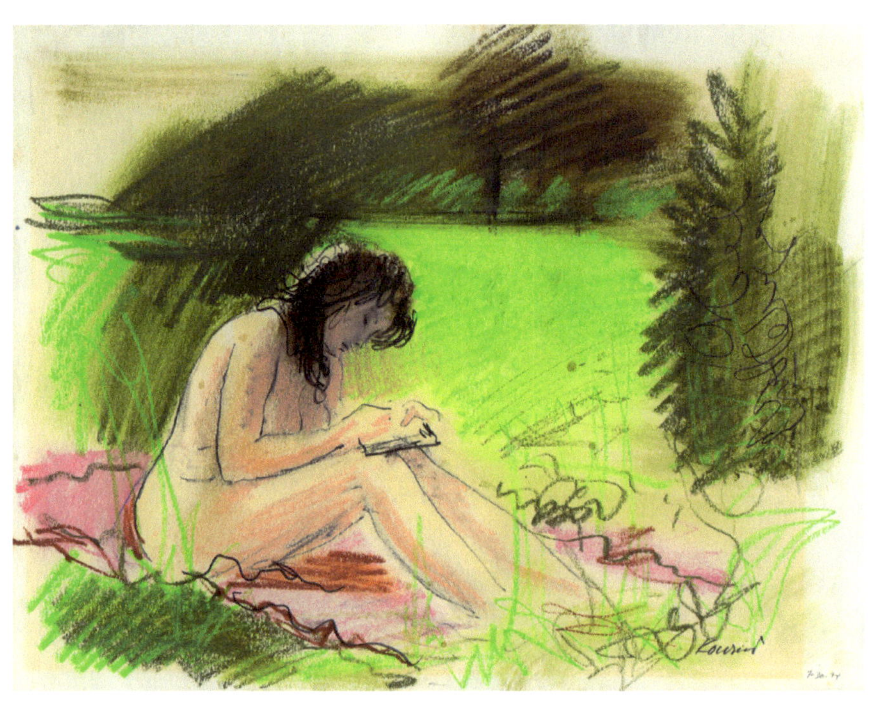

Writing Naked
> *for Adolf Konrad*

He was an artist who
could really capture clouds.
Those large romantic white ones
with all their shadowed roundness
floating weatherless against
Canaletto blue, forever.

He even created paintings full
of those clouds on Magritte high ceilings
holding an elaborate chandelier
in these strange Victorian houses
he was known for.
Each front lawn a ghostly garage sale
of period furniture and family photographs
staring out at you.

And on those days when things look up
because I see that sky, recall
the beginning, his encouragement
that sketch of a warm afternoon
me posed, writing on his last rose
of summer blanket, hiding nothing.

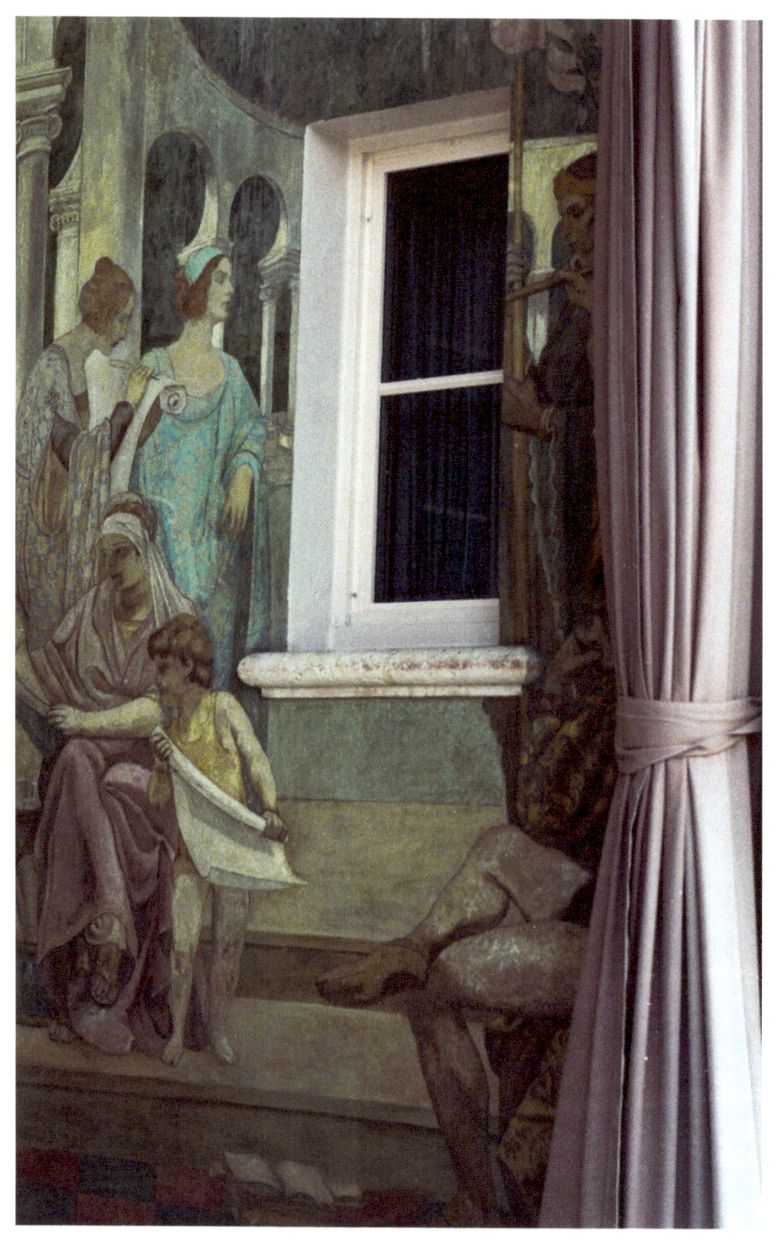

The Society of the Four Arts
Art-Music-Drama-Literature

Founded back in 1936 the building
has this large classic entry fresco
and they don't let just anyone join
after all, this is the Palm Beaches.

Membership is purposefully limited
to the number of seats in the auditorium.

We have all heard of a seat at the table,
the room where it happens,
but a seat in the auditorium
gives new meaning to the A list.

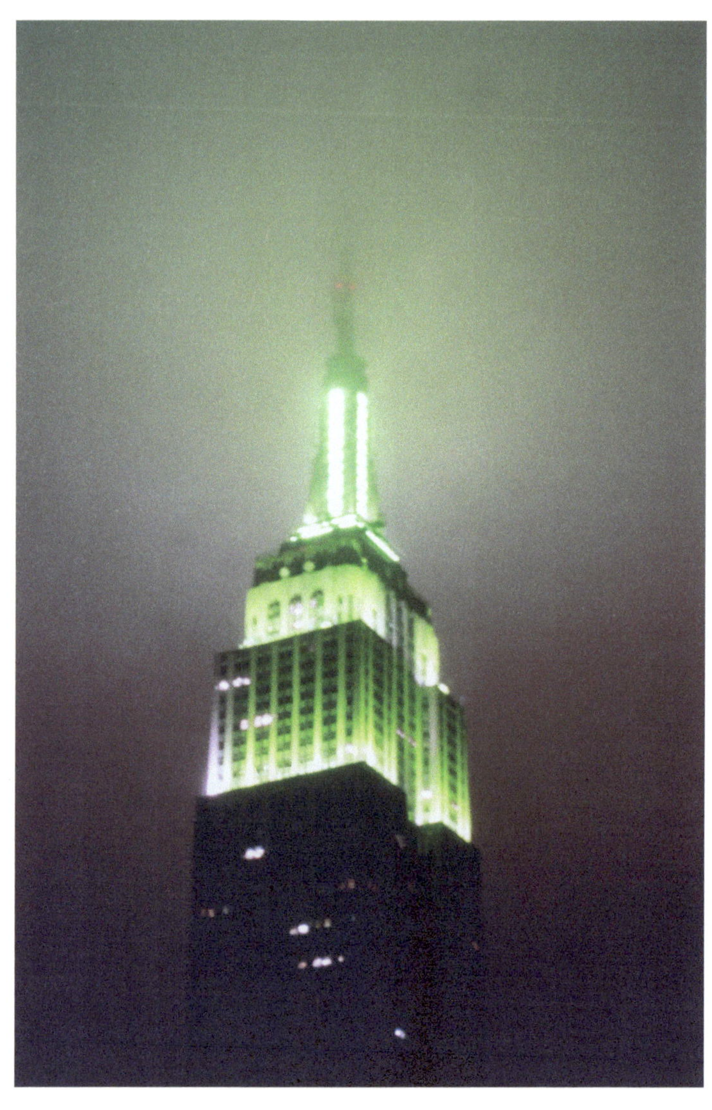

St. Patrick's Day

Winter has faded
the world-famous building glows
in a soft spring fog

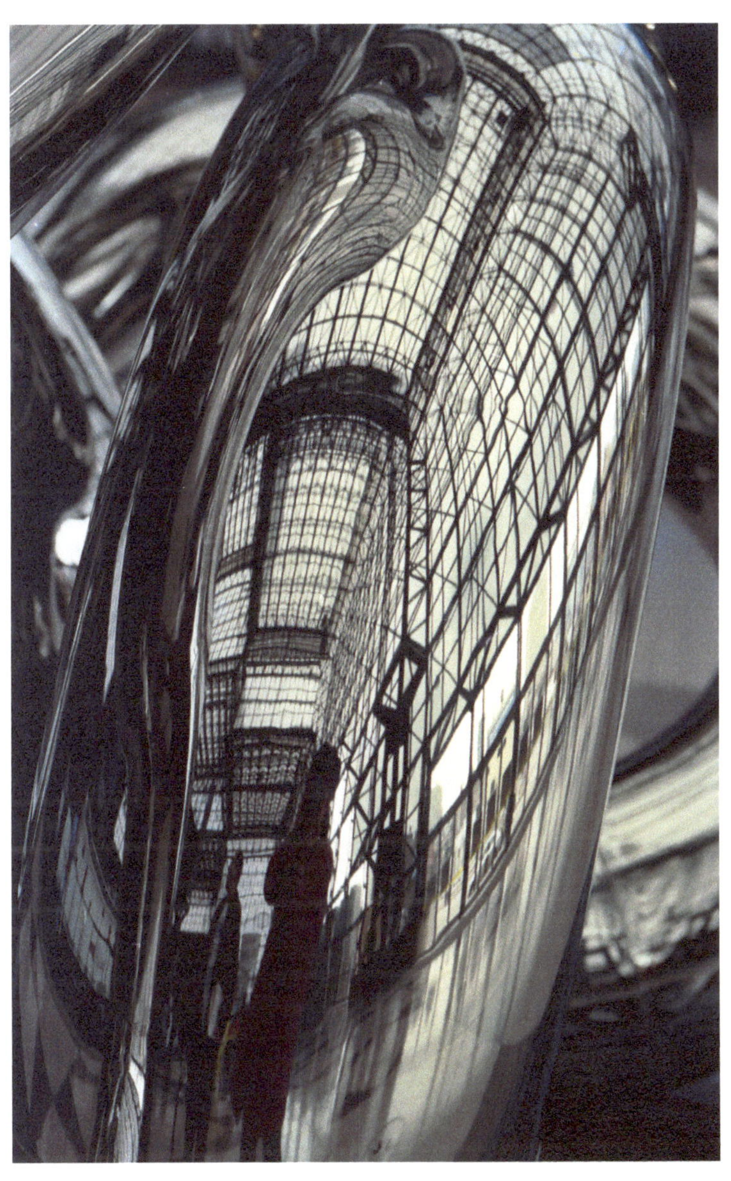

Chrome

A silver sculpture
twists an atrium's angles
coiling my image

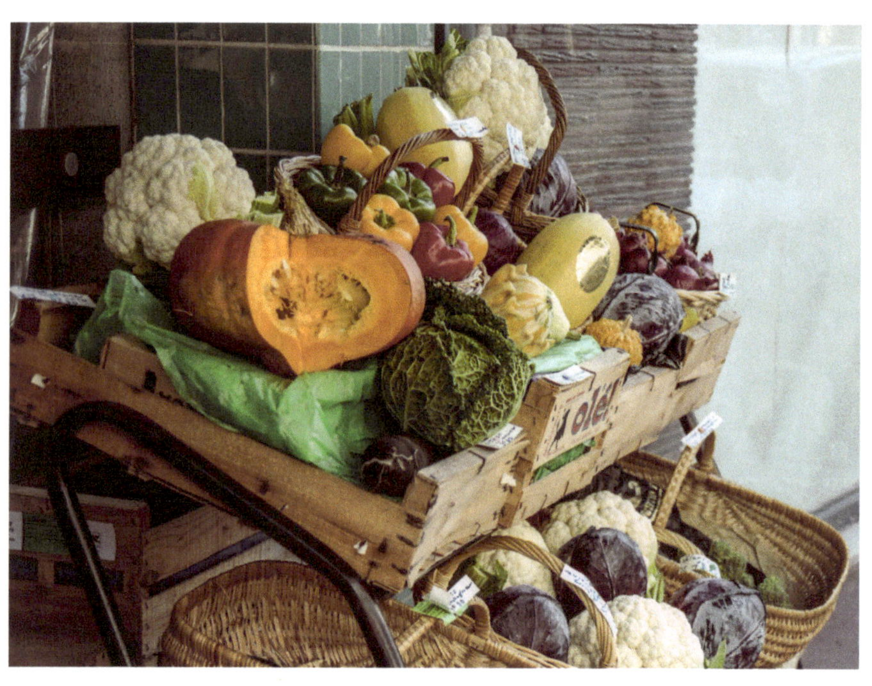

olé!

Bon Appetit

It is easy to throw dinner parties when you have lived
in a house with nine for dinner every night.

My Irish mother from Brooklyn thought potatoes two
vegetables
and a boiled meat was cuisine.

My Irish father, from Tennessee, adventurous, knew spices
could kill, dress and smoke all manner of meats.

The *more the merrier* was the mantra of our home, and
should too many drop by, it was *FHB* (family holds back).

So, I have a Holiday Soup Party for forty or more,
St Patrick's Day with corned beef and cabbage for a crowd.

A pot luck pasta party gathered round the pool,
a Halloween Party with freaky finger foods.

Over the years we have opened walls for better flow
with a pantry that could put on *Babette's Feast.*

I have neatly filed recipe clippings in loose-leaf binders
that I couldn't cook in three lifetimes.

Yet with memories of laughter rising, the wine flowing
let's check out that new issue of *Cooking Light.*

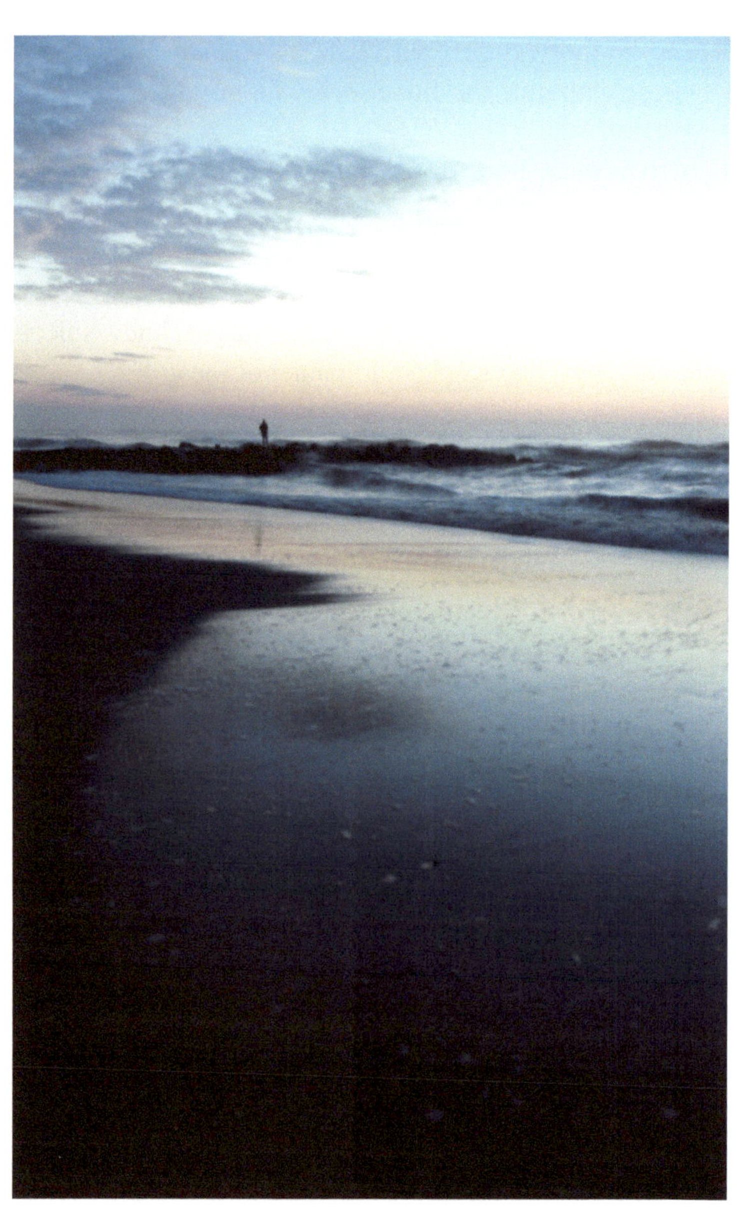

Sunrise, Montauk

Reason and sense remove anxiety
not houses that look out upon the sea.
                                    Montaigne

The waves say we are always
coming and leaving and like thought
cannot be caught or weighed
only felt, like the edge
of emptiness in the cry of a gull.

When it starts
that soft glow, then soon
a light you can't look at
rises from a shimmering sea
of lapis, emerald, onyx
out to edge of the earth.

The tide is out.
Fishermen cast lines
like spider webs into the wind
and darting birds run earnestly
along a white edged beach
while the missing moon
slowly moves the sea
closer to my chair.

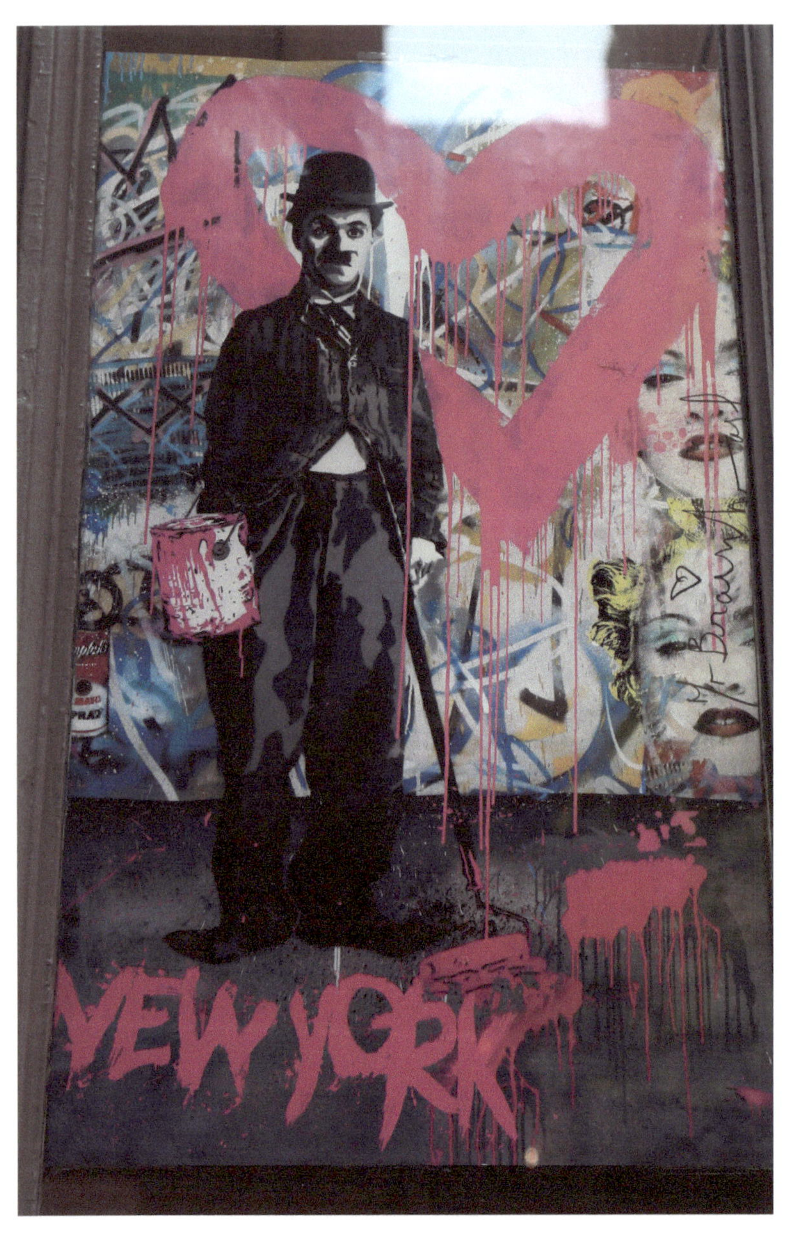

NEW YORK

Graffiti

For Banksy

We are the nobodies
writers with secret names
our *tags* clandestine as we
light our lines in the darkness
playing a rebellious fame game
with our folk art of the streets.

The illusive bane of authority
we fill up empty places
across the demi-monde,
have reached fine gallery walls.

They check my age
when I buy spray paint.

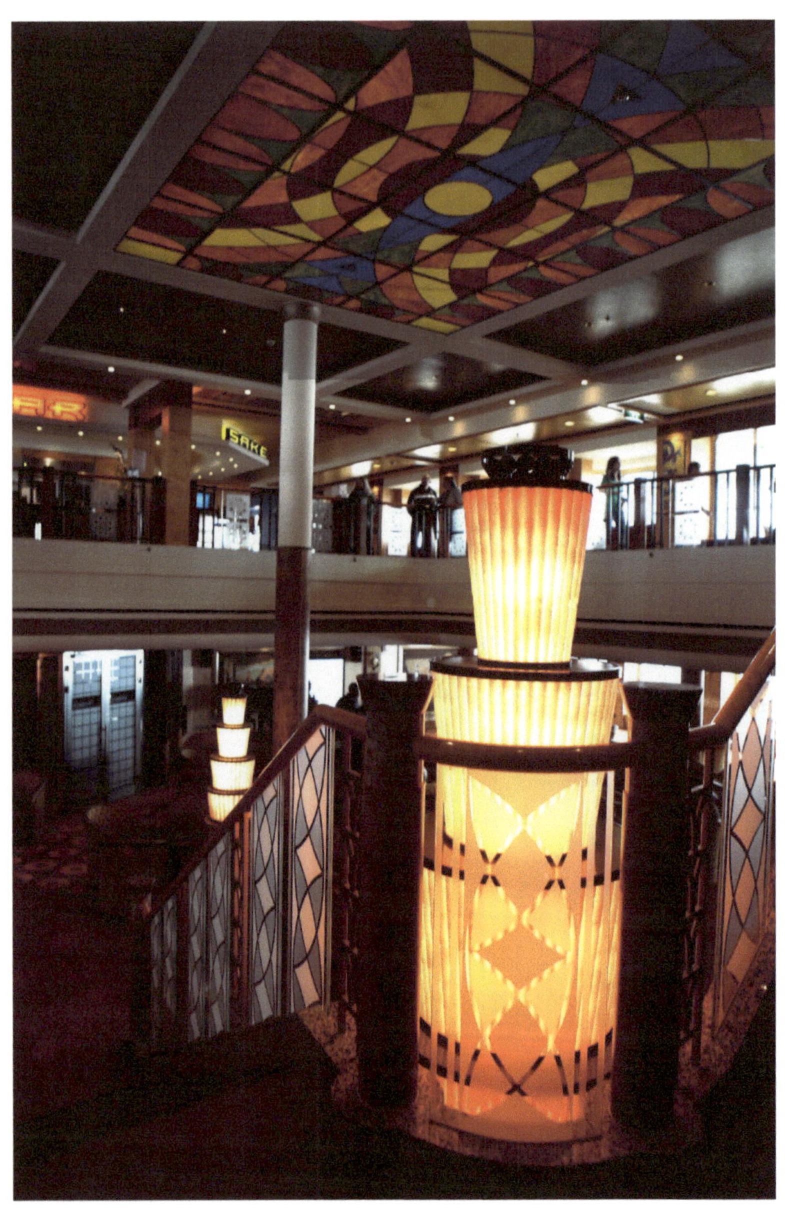

First Cruise

We leave Seattle, the Space Needle,
Pike Place Market, and Mt. Rainier.
Our ship, a small city of thousands
sails north into the cloud-shrouded
wildness of whales and glaciers.

On grand staircases, in the many
bars, restaurants, masses are at play,
dressed for the Caribbean,
on their way to Alaska.

And you realize
this is not your party.

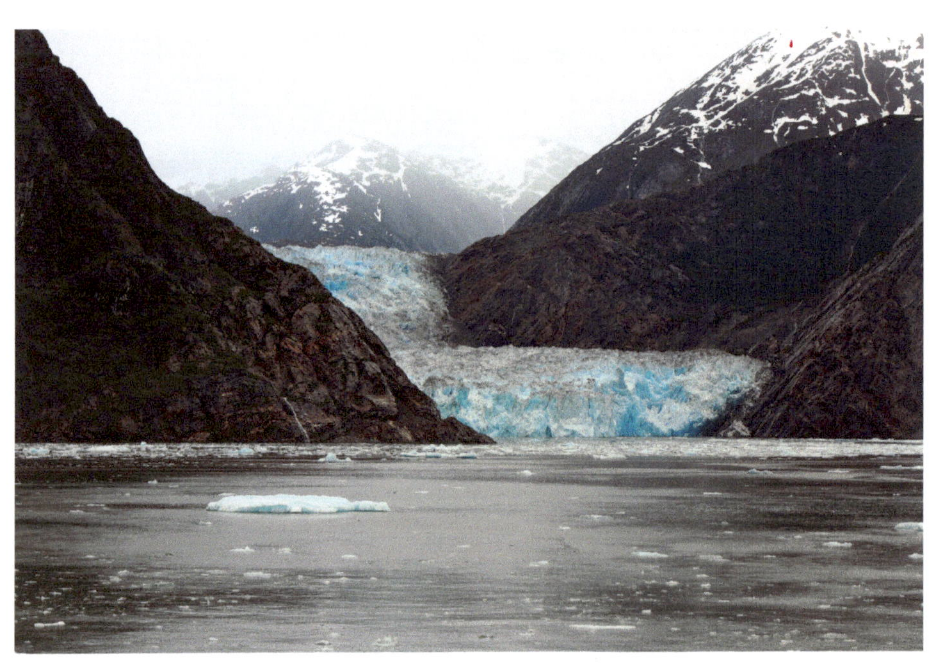

Sawyer Glacier - 2014

We are north in Alaska,
wrap wool scarves
around a long summer sun.
Sail out among volcanic spires
spilled into the sea, fill boats of watchers
come to see the breaching whales.
Evergreen forests cover the land
shelter elk, bear and eagle
along with year-round locals
tougher than their long dark winters.

The cruise ships loom ridiculous
in every tiny harbor, with towns
still nestled in another time,
they're roads, we learn, go nowhere.
But brightly painted totem poles
perch beside the parking lots
of busy tourist shops.

Then words just disappear as we
slow and glide into a narrow fjord;
the white debris of icebergs floating by
while endless lacy waterfalls
spill down the clouded cliffs.
We come upon a misty field of snow
flowing down a black rock canyon
that becomes a giant wall of
cracking bright blue ice.

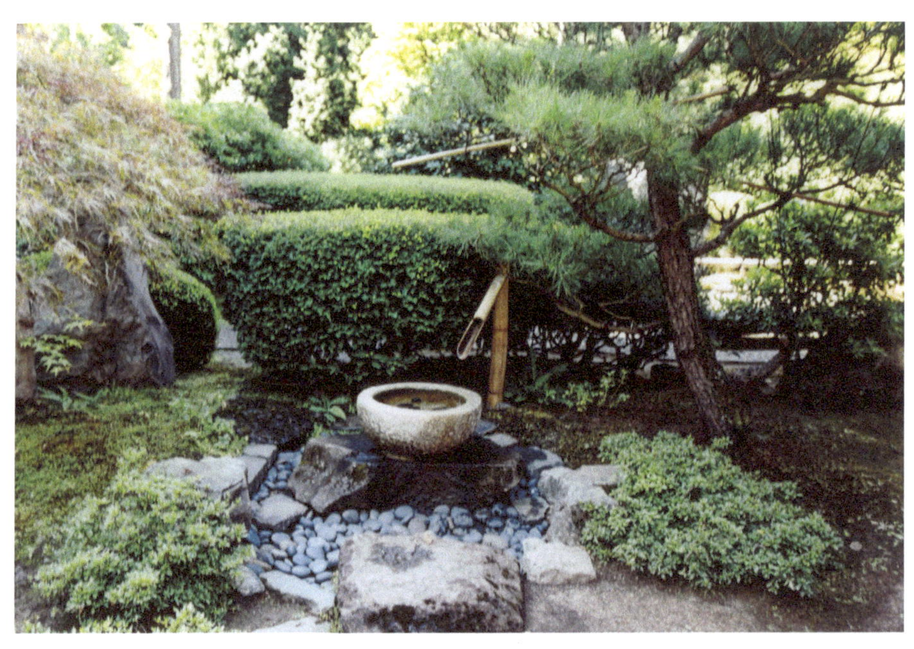

An Asian Garden

Each thoughtful design
a branch tied up or trimmed
tree - as work of art.

The old stone lantern
placed so - at the corner
in dappled shadows.

The curved red bridge
spans a gentle flowing stream.
Climb up and cross over.

Grooves in white gravel
round the sparsely spaced rocks.
A rake sits waiting.

Stepping stones aligned
pleasing necklace through a pool.
Walk on the water.

Smells of moss and fern
grace notes for this rich green earth.
Time to stop - breathe in.

This hollow bamboo
balanced over a stone bowl
slow dripping water.

Go down a new path
when a chance stone bench invites
come sit - pause your life.

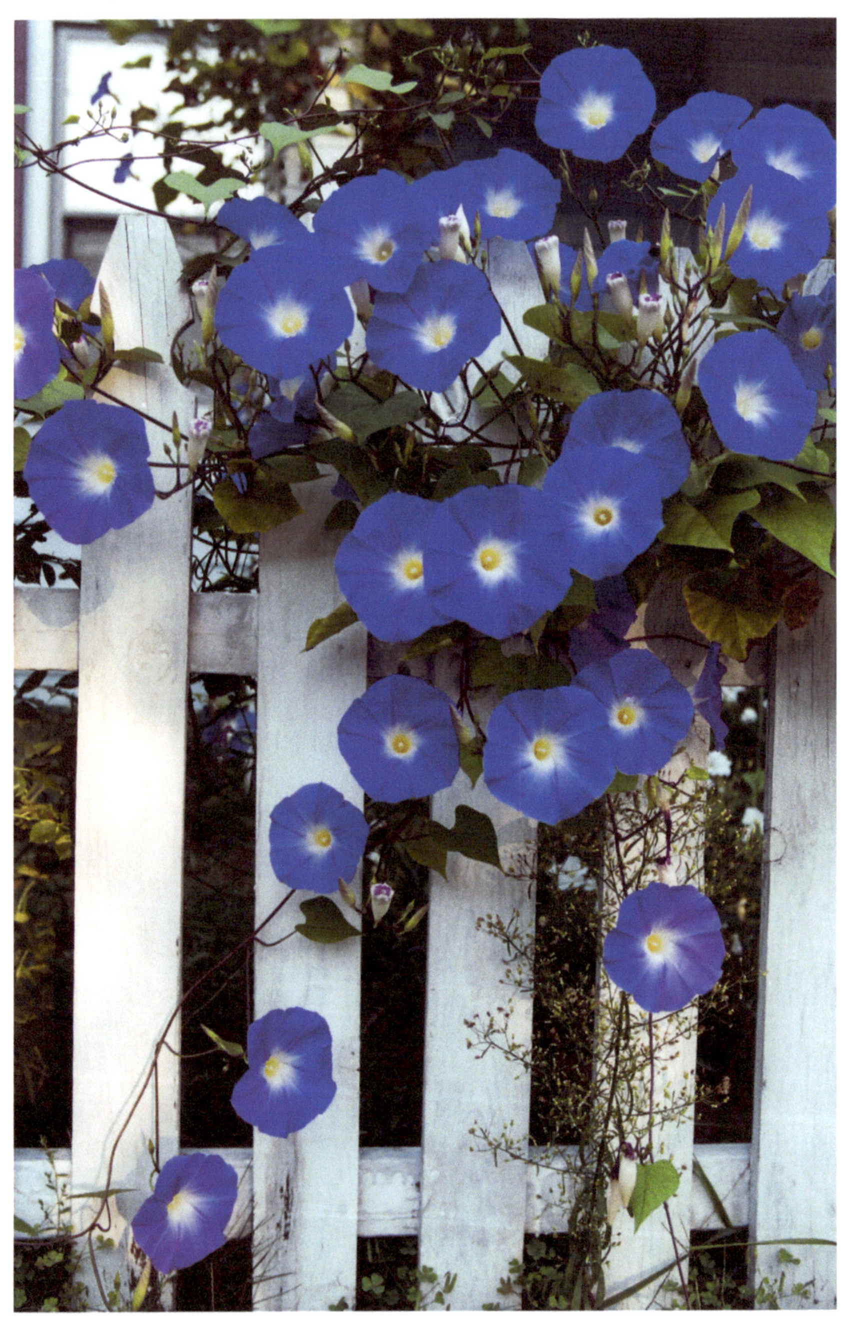

Off a Blue Sun

After Ada Limon

You give into your love
and lift its sunlight

above the sand. You stand up
from under what fixed you

harvest three crops
as a truth. One

for what will not die
like earth away from us.

One against what will not
starve and famish.

One for what will not
fly off and confuse us.

I am the flower.

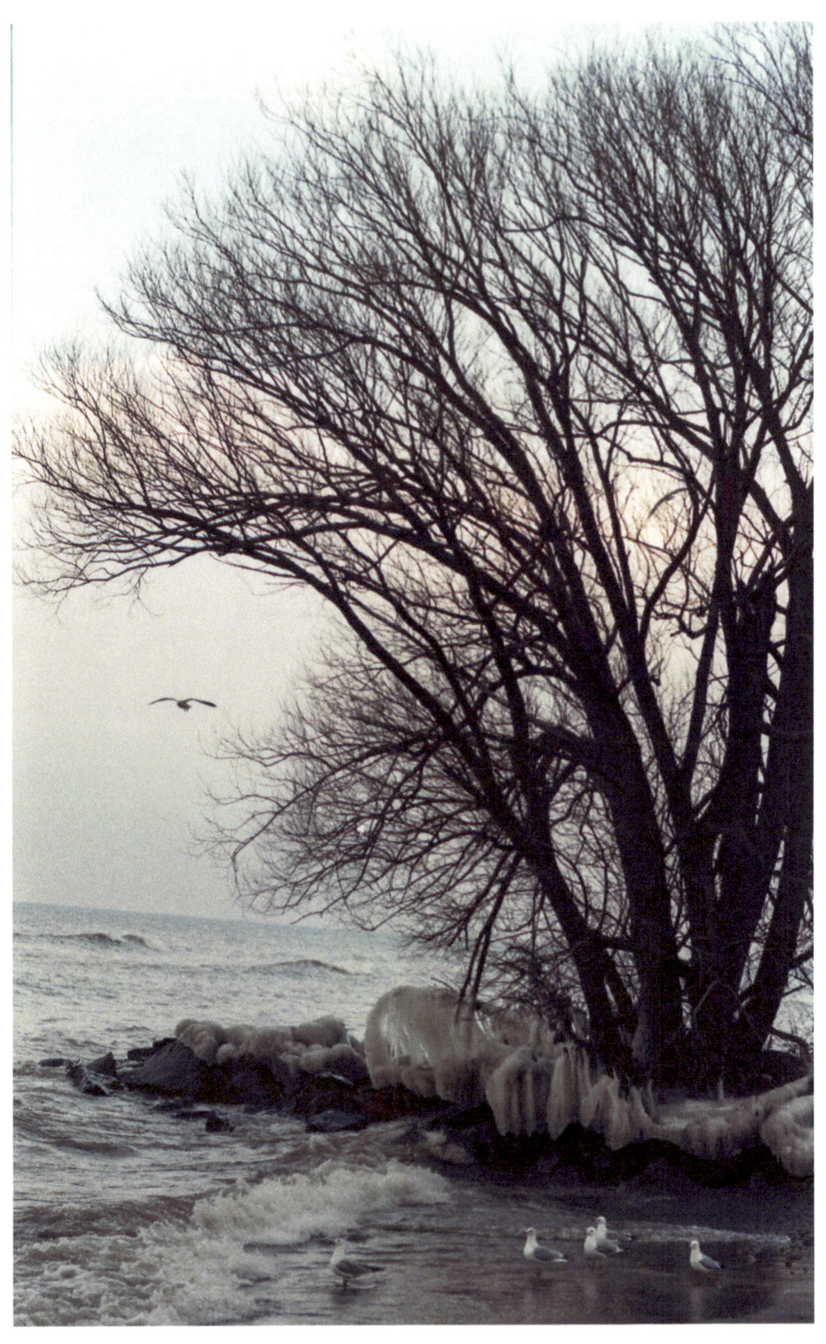

Solstice

after Emily Dickinson

I felt a wind come from the north
It shivered through the land
The air became so bitter cold
It froze the ungloved hand

Rain is sliding down the cold
On lake edge thick with ice
Daylight has its shortest breath
As we say winter thrice

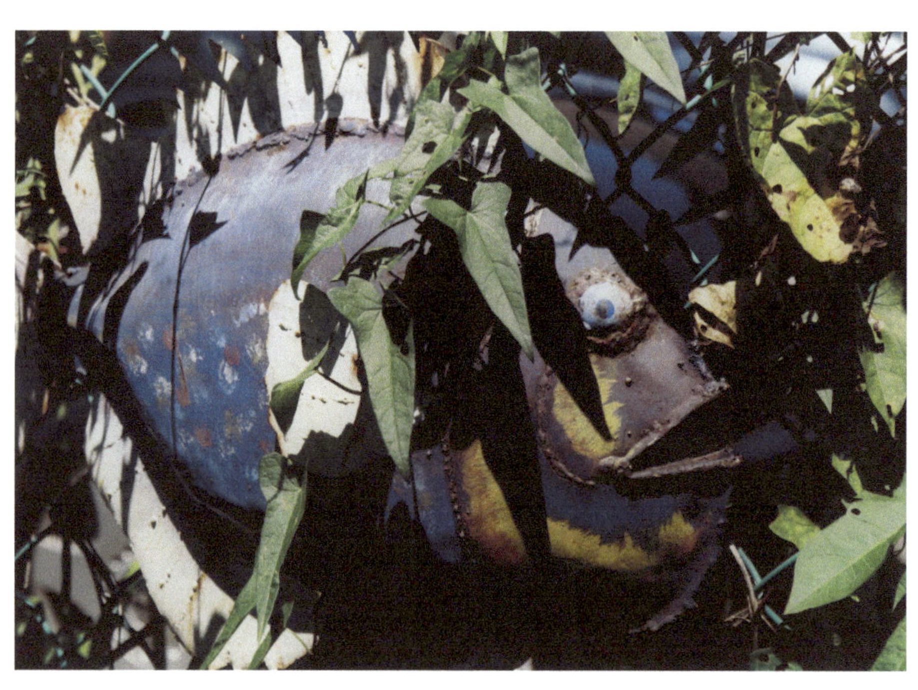

Nine Ways of Looking at Fish

after Wallace Stevens

There are fish swimming
all around my studio.

Fish are such silent creatures
perfectly useful for writers.

A sunset wind comes down from the Tetons.
Across Jackson Lake the fish are jumping.

The rolling waves slide up the beach.
We come from fish. We miss the sea.

A rainbow meant to chime the wind
drops down in a spiral of tiny glass fish.

Winter ice covers the stilled pond.
Silver fish sleep deep in the mud.

Aged twelve, I drop in my tangled line
and catch the prize trout. Fish story.

Storied stars, with facing fish, say Pisces people
will be important in your life.

Dragonflies dart about our garden pool.
Do the fish know the heron has come?

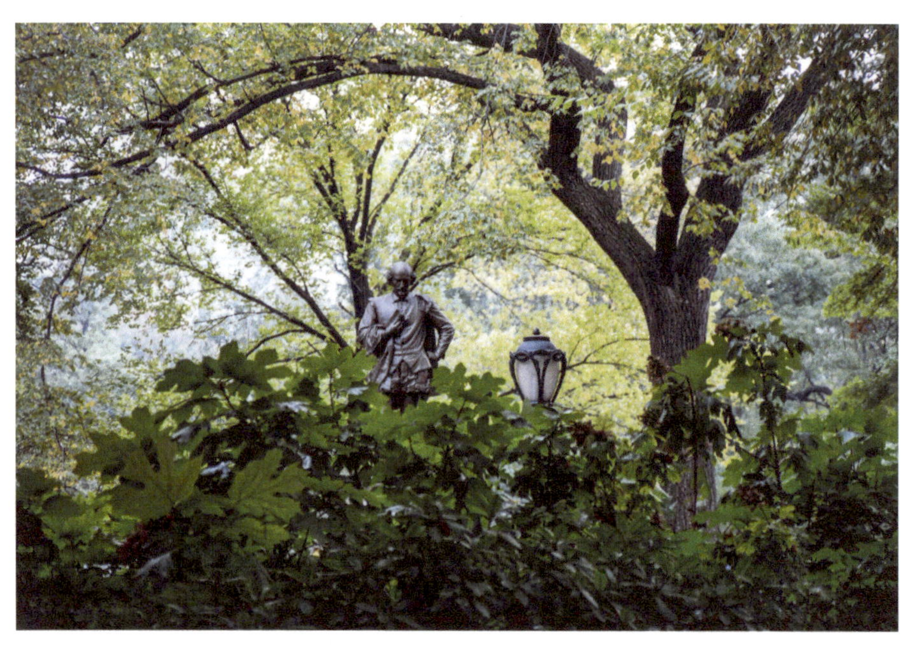

Shakespeare - Gone 400 Years

That thou upon the wastes of time have gone,
and we attend times leisure with a moan,
yet, still we wonder at your lexicon,
how on your writing moss has never grown.

As subject to time's love, or to time's hate
you did but hope your simple verse might stand.
Now all the world does call your writing great
full human nature in its wise command.

Thou, by the dial's shady stealth now know
time's thievish progress to eternity;
and gates of steel so strong, yet time cuts low,
but ink exists for all posterity.

For as the Sun, is daily new and old,
so is your love still telling what is told.

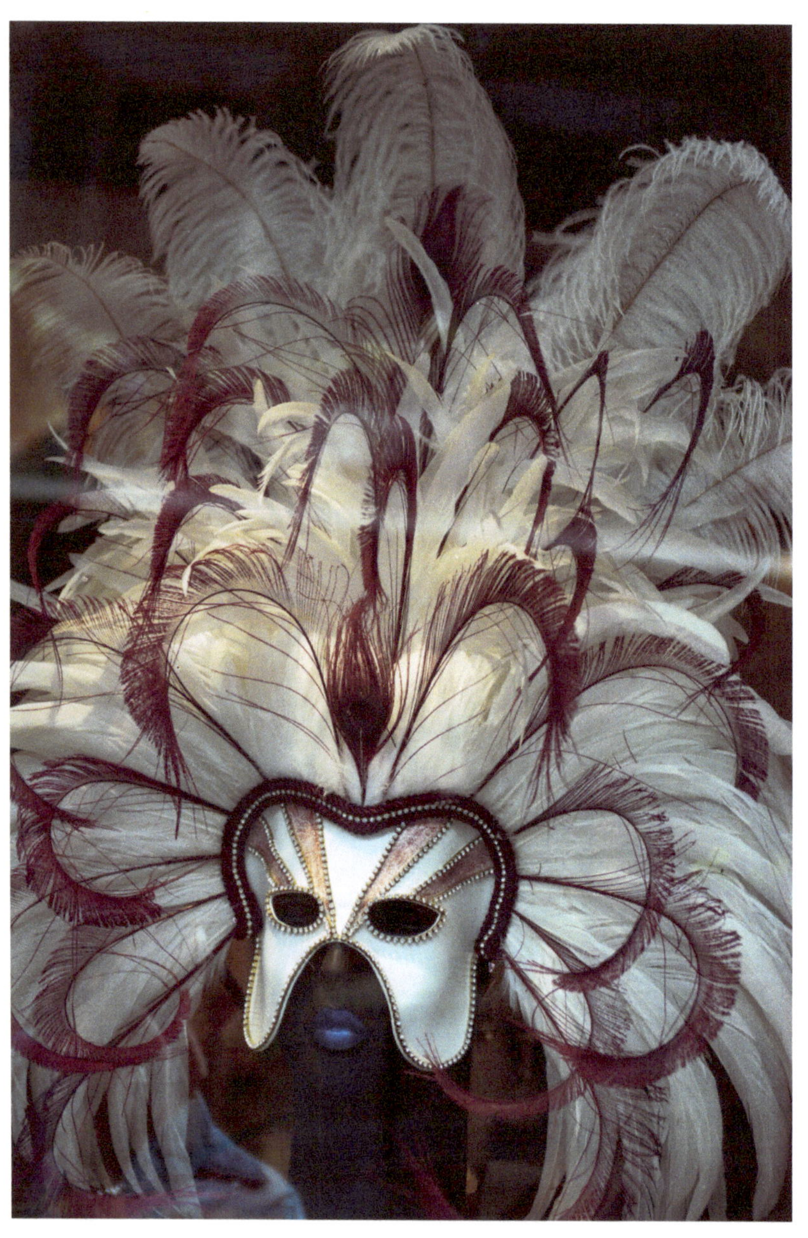

New Orleans

You old riverboat city where the
Mississippi bends with waters
from the bayous sliding by.
Your snaking iron railings lure us
down worn cobbled streets to
where strange graveyards
shelve and box their bones.

Tourists' clopping surreys
pass the long and shadowed alleys
where fountained inner sanctums
are hidden from the street.
You're the *Big Easy,* you laugh
calliope, swallow shipping
and sing the blues.

Your *Vieux Carre* blasts jazz
to let the good times roll
as the natives toss glances
like Mardi Gras necklaces
and pungent Cajun spices
blow from busy kitchens
while a black boy on the corner
taps out his life behind
a hat full of coins.

At Toulouse and Chartres
we sit and eat our gumbo
with night-life moving past
wide open doors. A man
tucked in the corner

worn out as his clothes
holds a conversation with himself.

High up, new glass and steel
look down upon it all.
We people - like the boats
come and go.

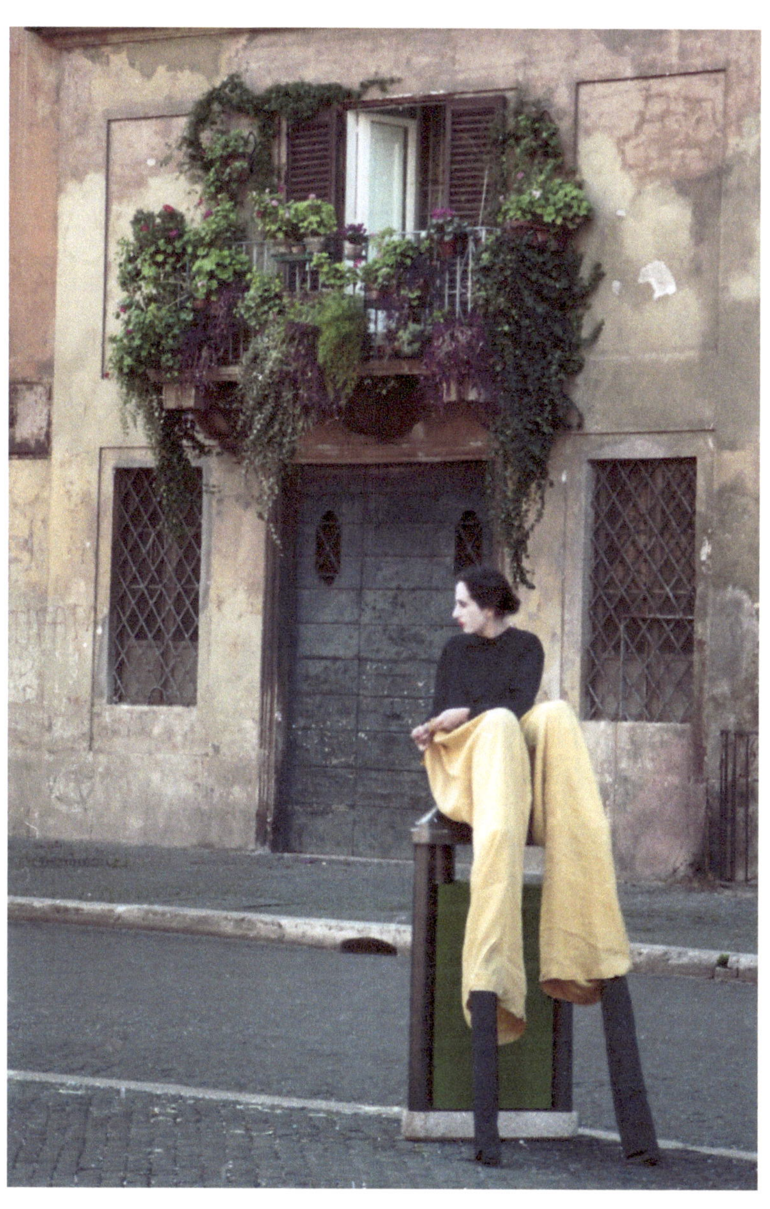

Piazza Navona

The street stilt walker
readies without a backstage
has her own strange show

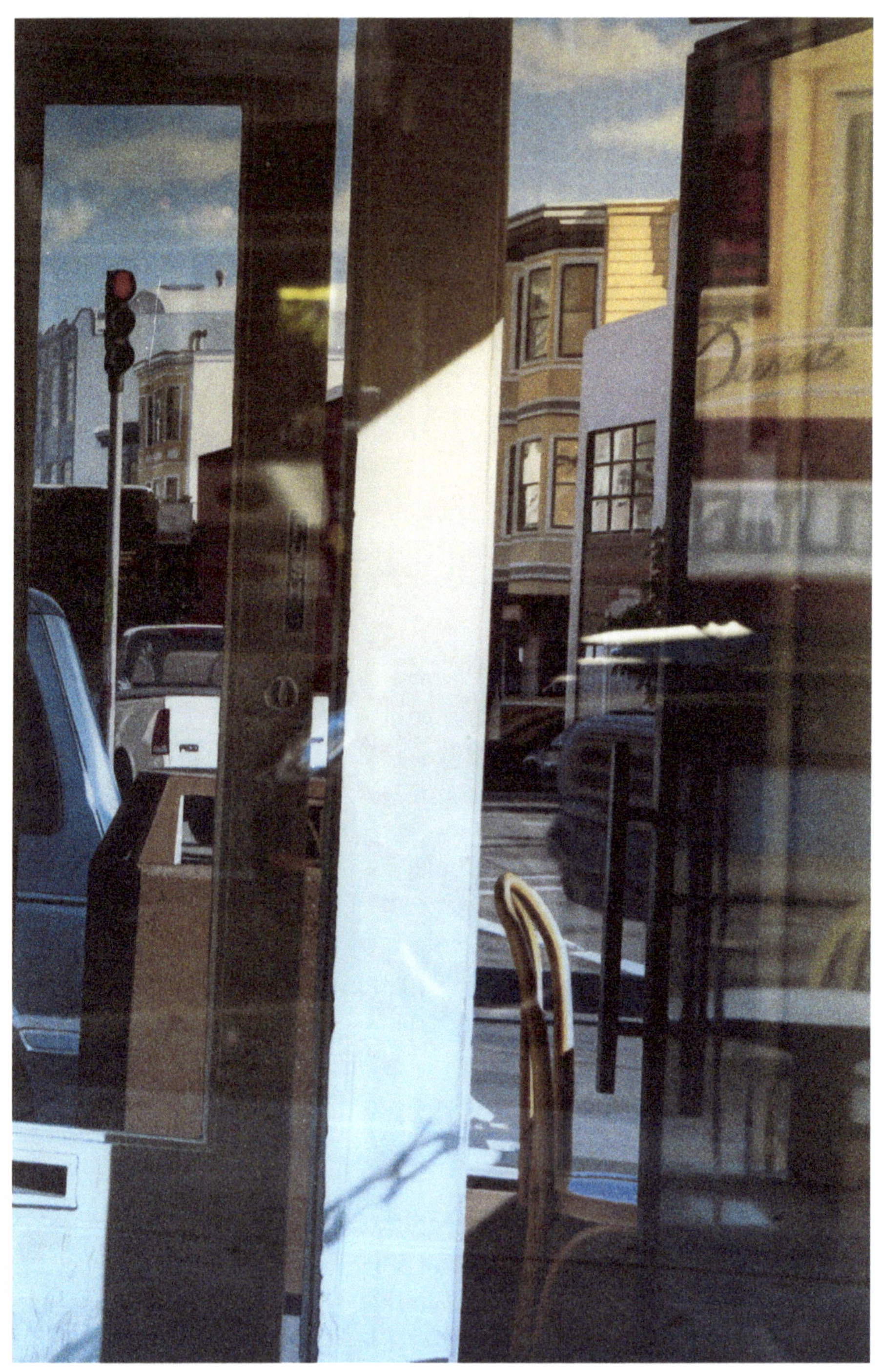

Pacific Heights

You will grow fit on these hills
where sidewalks morph into stairs.

In this neighborhood
persons of note reside
in stately *painted ladies*,
possess sweeping views
of San Francisco Bay.
Their posh boutiques and
smart cafes line Filmore.

Enjoying my early morning coffee
I shoot from an open door
fracturing the street.

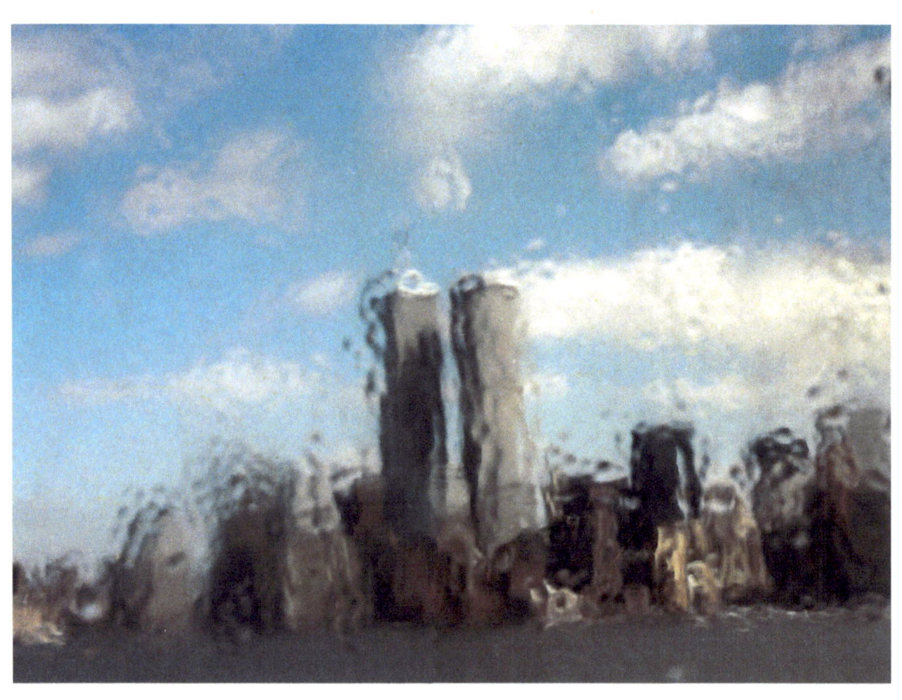

Planes in the Sky

The sky is crazy high above our house
sitting under an approach to Newark Airport.
On busy afternoons the planes fly in circles. At sunset
long contrails mingle with the pink and purple clouds.

And there are times I look up and wonder
where do all these people come from;
giving their heart to sales calls in San Francisco,
that dream vacation, so *We'll always have Paris*
a visit to children *Rocky Mountain High* near Denver?

Then it comes, the memory of that September
when for three days all our skies went empty
and later when the acrid smoke drifted
from lower Manhattan over the beach
where I walked alone on the Jersey Shore.
Our group would soon gather at sunset
as we do each Rosh Hashanah to share food
go around the table and tell about our year.

Now each September the city pauses
somber people gather on a plaza
twin waterfalls pouring into the void
for the reading of the names.

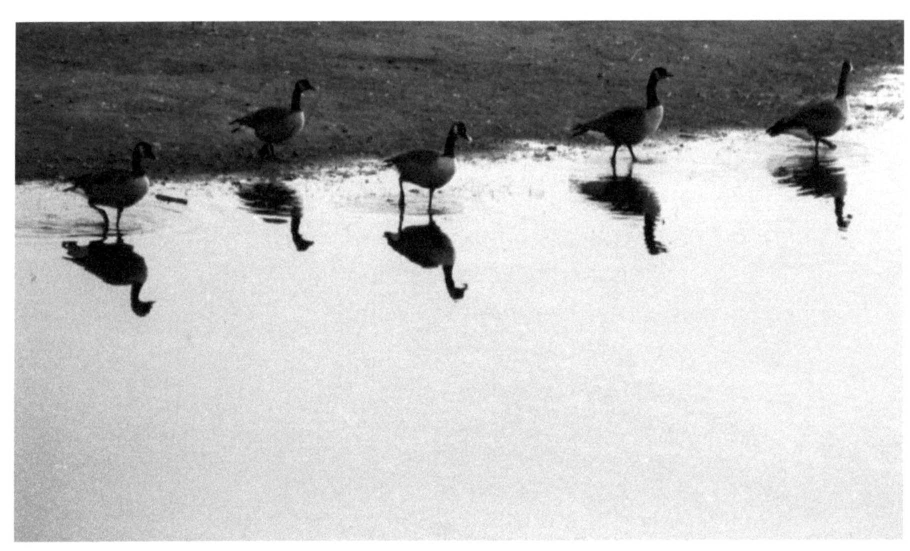

Meanwhile

after Mary Oliver

Our world offers itself
to your imagination.
Do you ponder your place
in the family of things?

Consider, *Wild Geese.*

Or has some accident of birth
tucked you away from imagination;
safe on your knees in a dogma
with infallible answers
creating infidels, goyim, heathens
in our family of things.

Meanwhile, out to the edge of time,
billions of suns twinkle in the night.

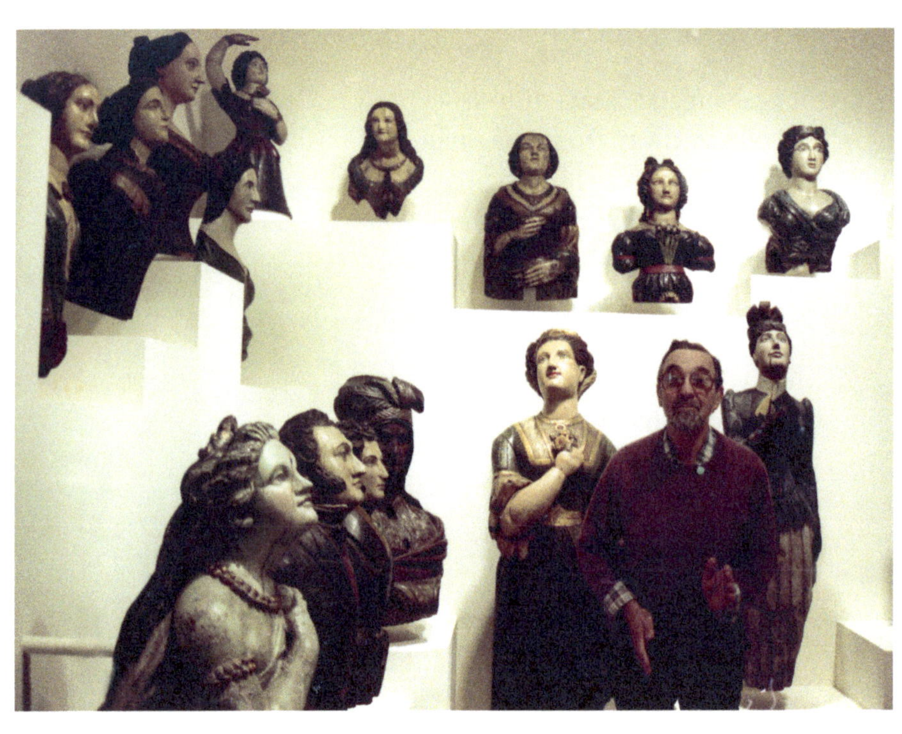

This Marriage

You, just six months younger than my mother
rainbowed in through a sea of beige leisure suits
in your open purple-navy-red flecked shirt
and I thought, *Who the hell is this flake?*

Stalking, you circled and came in
dumping gin in my lap. And I listened
to your story, older than language,
new as a flower that bloomed in that night
seeking a companion, not a conquest.

Could it be possible?
No, I already had one husband, two children, three cats,
a lover - and was President of the PTA,
plus, you lived too far away.
This was in June.

Our breath steams heavy in the swirling sweat of August
and you would drive two hours
to meet me in a diner for linguini lunch.
Leaves were aflame when we stopped walking
on the ground and any eyes that caught us knew.

Then it was the cloudy November kitchen,
as the love triangle sat facing round our hard rock
maple table because you must always try to save
the marriage. But you broke the rules, called early
and I couldn't hear the words you were saying
a falling elevator whispering in my head,
You fool this is the one, the one thought not possible!

After the bells ring and the ball drops for a New Year
I take young children from their beds, their schools,
their father.

And my Mother says, *He looks so Jewish!*
I leave three apple trees, my two-car garage,
one lover and the PTA to live
in four upstairs rooms next to a highway.
Family, friends wait in stunned pity for the fall.

But after these many years, my love
the teasing laugh of your mind still catches me
rounding the corners of our memories.

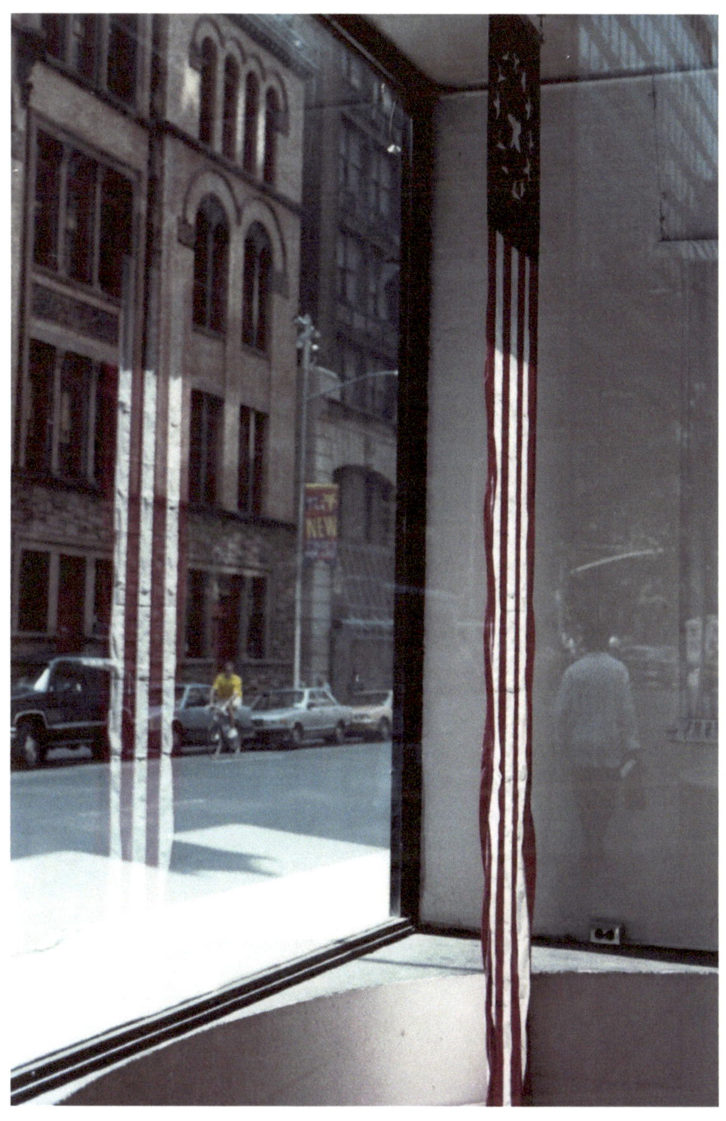

Coming and Going

Narrow hanging flag,
glowing in the city scene
coming and going

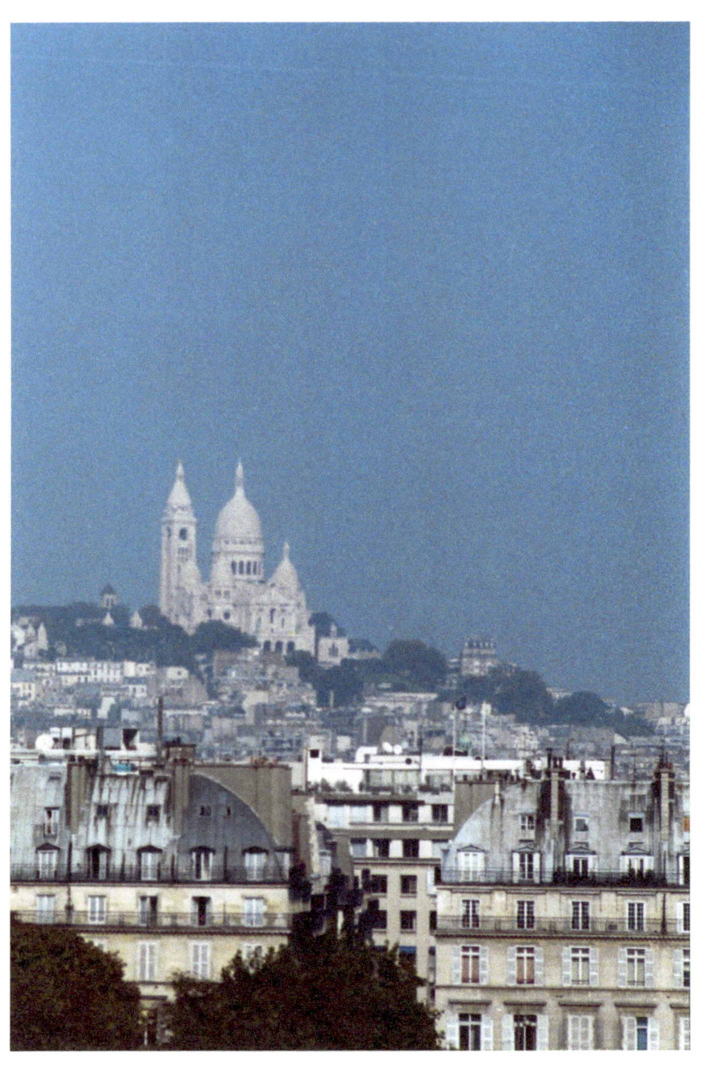

We'll Always Have Paris
for Marvin

We were a cliché
the older man   young wife

You   roared out in the twenties
me mid-World War II   Yet oddly

during both our younger days
we fall in love   with the same movies

you at the cinema palaces   for me
called classics   on the small screen

And you had those   soft blue words
that could pick any lock

I knew   I was in trouble
on those curves   in the dark

But then   ah well   you know the rest
Could always honestly say

Here's looking at you kid!

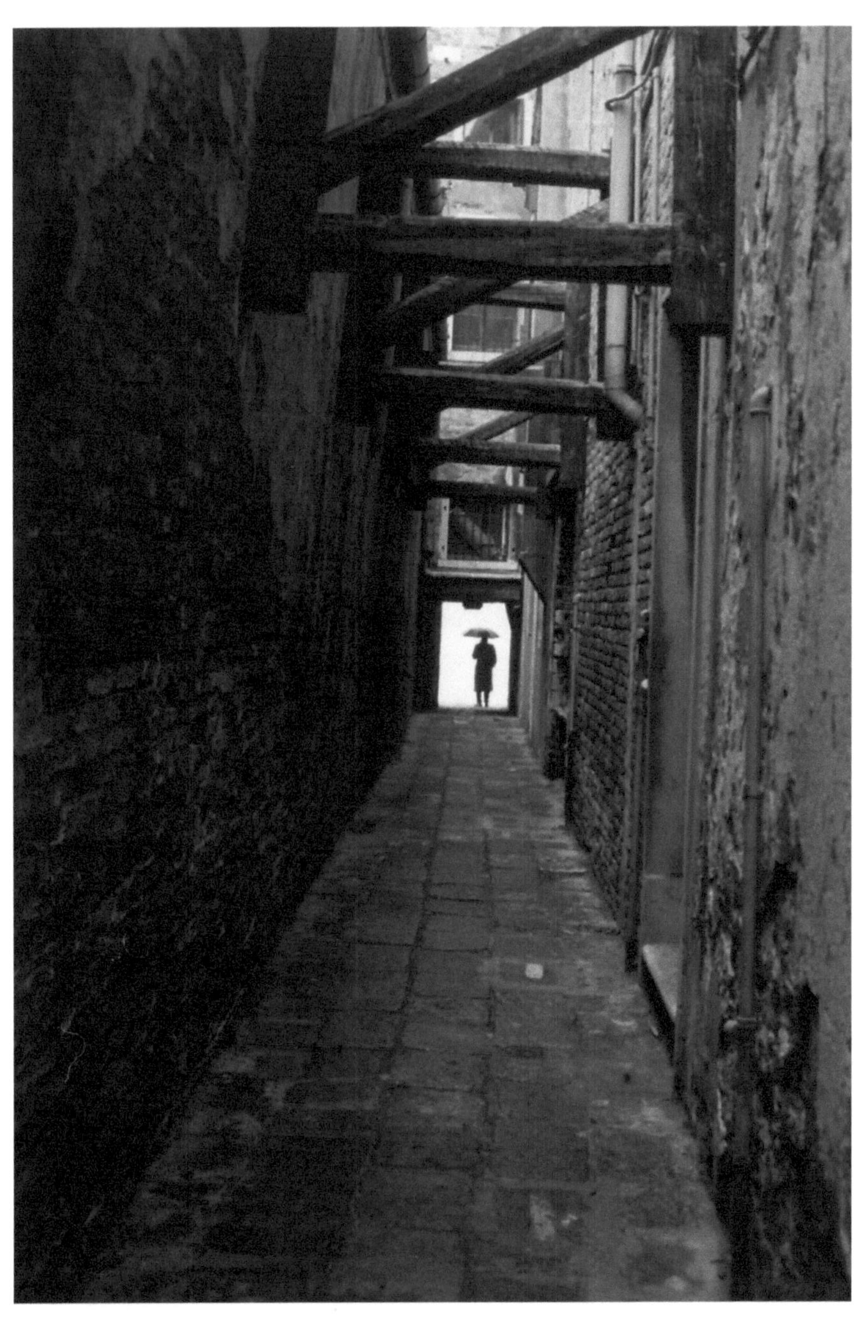

Infinity

I seek out long converging lines
that vanish in, draw you out
of this aging Venetian alley
needing timbers now
to hold medieval walls.

My husband standing
patient in the rain
for I have stopped again
to grab another shot.
I yell to him down the alley
Don't move!
And there he stands
in infinity.

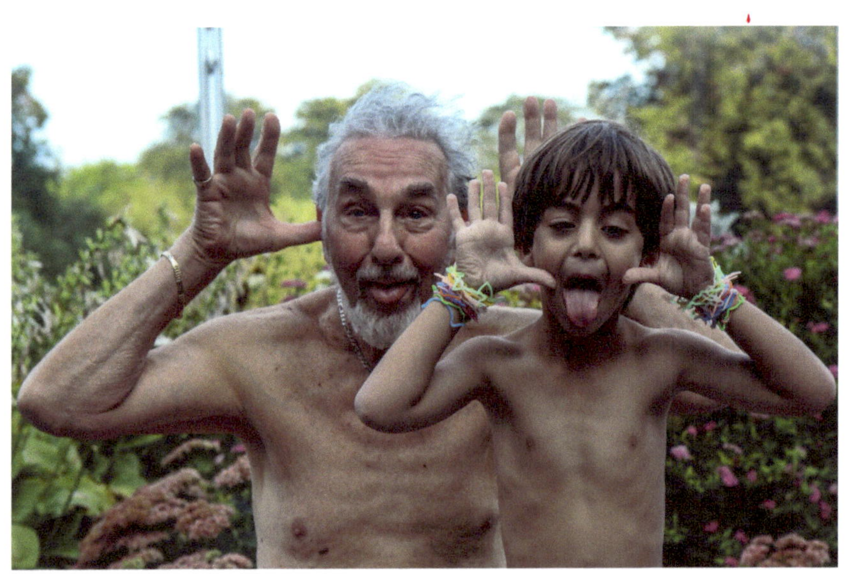

Lightening Up

You died of time itself,
it's what we wish for.

I threw out your days of the week,
each one with a lid for all the pills
to keep your heart from failing.

You know your twin grandsons,
tall like their mountains, fit into many
of the clothes you left behind.
They filled your big burgundy suitcase
and carried them away to Colorado.

We donated those hulking black recliners.
A light urban grey now softens the room
you spent so much time in.

You would love that I chose
the picture from Chicago, the one
with you and Nael blowing raspberries,
to place in front of the plain black
metal box on the dresser.

No matter our terrain
we could always make each other laugh.

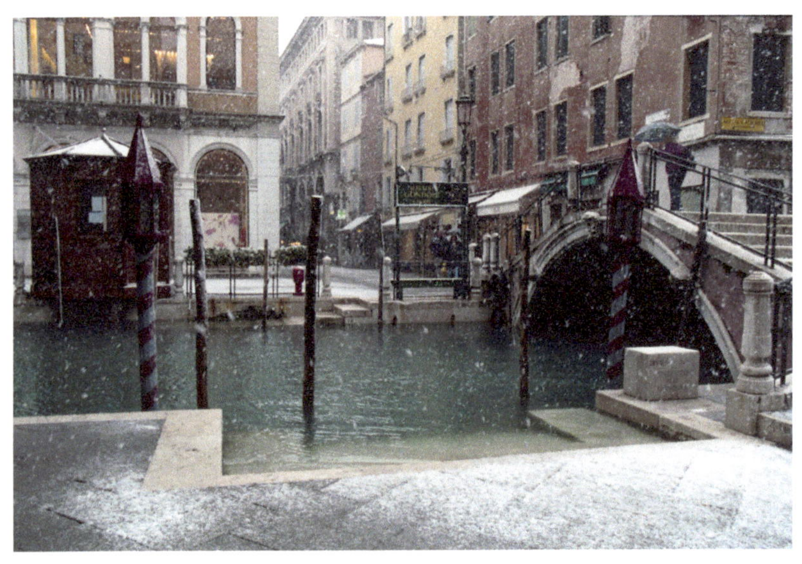

For the Good Times

Now with only flashbacks, the weight of truth,
create stories while you can, the ones
you return to like a tongue to a missing tooth.

Remember my first flight, the laws of physics
pushing me back, you are holding my hand;
that Sunday morning in Savannah circling the squares,
where they invented historic preservation,
Nina Simone singing *Sunday Morning in Savannah.*

Remember you pointing out Chuck Close in his wheelchair
speaking with Phillipe DeMontebello because Kiki Smith
had invited us worker bees to her opening at MoMA; or
that gangly elderly man full of music scat dancing with
Lionel Hampton on a portable stage as we cuddled on
the ground in a New Brunswick pocket park.

Remember the *Big Easy* suddenly serious at 10 pm
on a Saturday night when all the police cars stopped
dead in the street, the police just walking away;
or those goosebumps, her regalia right out of Star Wars,
as we all jumped cheering to our feet, Martha Graham
had walked on stage and we are there like yesterday.

Remember sharing a perfect roast chicken from a brown
paper bag that Indian summer afternoon on the
vineyard's rock wall in St. Emilion; or seeing Kathy Bates,
that final gunshot in *Night Mother*, the entire audience
filing out like from a tomb.

Remember embracing in wonder alone on the beach at
Montauk under a moonless night, the swish of Milky Way;
and all the side-splitting laughter when we would write -
perform those silly parodies for someone's life event

with our circle of friends, the *Usual Suspects*

Remember walking out after Madeline Albright spoke
onto the broad white marble terrace of the State
Department, that long summer sunset over Washington;
and our hilarity when your improvised Hora won the dance
contest at a raucous pub in Killarney.

Remember you close to eighty climbing ancient cliff
ladders clinging to the edge of Mesa Verde;
our laughing breathless pauses resting on the switchback
trail out of Crater Lake; and of course, when it snowed in
Venice, holding us in that magical white dusted day.

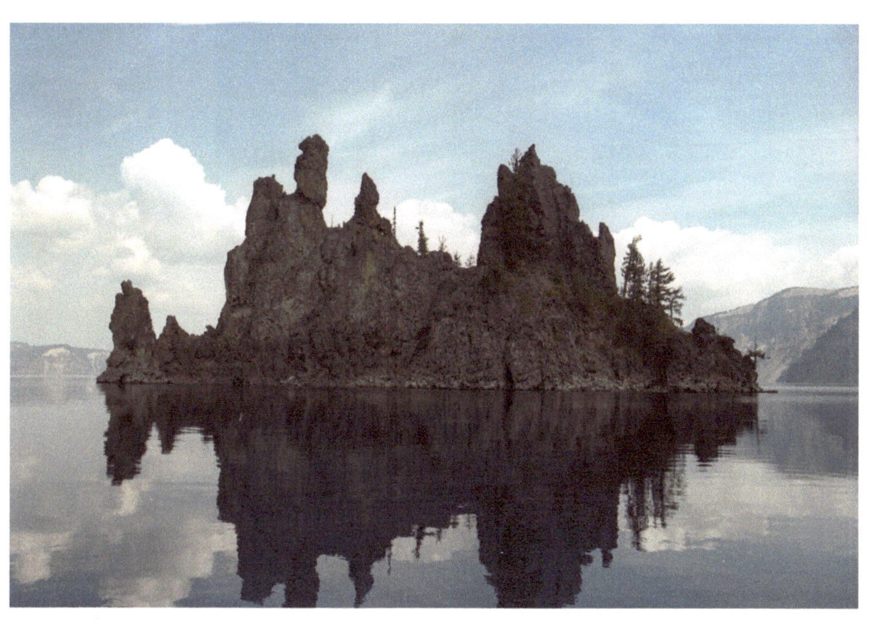

Crater Lake

Switchback trail down the caldera
to a lake without a river
our boat glides on clearest water
and we understand what deep is

Acknowledgements

I have been fortunate to have had some of these photographs recognized in regional exhibits:
Fashion and *Society of the Four Arts*, First Prize, the American Society Media Photographers-NJ
Pacific Heights, Patrons Award, Phillips Mill Photography Exhibit
Window Dressing, Purchase Prize, Mercer County Photography Exhibit
Graffiti, Crimson Atelier Award, Best in show, Merck, Union County
Rubbish, Award of One Person Show, Watchung Arts Center

A few of my poems have appeared in the following anthologies, in earlier versions.
The Anthologist, New Orleans; *A Different Latitude*, Civilities

I can never thank enough, Professor, Alicia Suskin Ostriker, who first set me on the path of poetry, and to Mark Doty, whose several workshops and pointed feedback affirmed I was on the right path. I would not have come this far without the US1 Poet's Cooperative critique group, The Delaware Valley Poets, and the Osher Lifelong Learning Institute, Rutgers University.

I wish to thank my many serious and thoughtful readers who helped early on and throughout the long development of this book. First the "Usual Suspects" Elena Stolzer, Aura Star and Esther Rouder whose job was to eliminate what was not working. Gyuri Hollosy, for his visual sensibilities, and my tell it like it is sister, Lynn Brown. My deepest gratitude to our Four Friends Poetry group whose careful editing and pointed questions were invaluable, Enriqueta Carrington, Ilene Millman, and especially Maxine Sussman, whose excellent workshops over these past years have led to many of these poems.

My serious gratitude to the team at PrintPOD Publishing, Jacqueline Flamm, Michael Aslett, and Kymberly Rosenthal for their knowledge and design skills that shaped very rough material into a book to be proud of.